Mrs. C's Economics with Ease

A Workbook for *"Macroeconomics"*

Diamond Huang
H115093

Marilyn Cottrell
Brock University

KENDALL/HUNT PUBLISHING COMPANY
4050 Westmark Drive   Dubuque, Iowa 52002

second midterm
ch 22, 23, 24.

Cover image by Robert Gemmell

Dedication

To my wonderful husband, Alan, and my five beautiful children, Warren, Ian, Stuart, Rylan, and Ashleigh, five of whom chose to take at least one economics course to better understand my great love of economics. To Ian and Ashleigh, who chose economics as their major without regret. To my son Warren, who has always given me a special strength, understanding, and dedication in all that I do. Lost, but never forgotten. For your love and support, I will be eternally grateful.

Love grows as a family expands. To the joyous additions and love of my ever-growing family: Nicole, Ian's wife; Melissa, Stuart's wife; Michal, Rylan's wife; and Adam, Ashleigh's fiancé. Thank you for the happiness you bring to dad and to me.

Dana
dm06wy @ brocku.ca

PL420.
Office Hours: M. W.
12:00 - 1:00.

CONTENTS

*Note: This text follows the chapters in *Macroeconomics*, Eleventh Canadian Edition, by Richard G. Lipsey and Christopher T. S. Ragan.

Acknowledgments

I would like to thank my colleagues, Professors Robert Dimand and Lewis Soroka of Brock University, for their invaluable assistance and guidance in not only this, but in many other scholarly endeavours. Special thanks to Karen Phillips our administrative assistant and veritable wonder-woman for her valuable technical support.

Q2. P47~63.

To Macroeconomics Students

Success in economics need not be elusive. Understanding the basic concepts of economics and the ability to do very straightforward problems will lead you, the student, to success in economics. Once you have mastered the basic problems, any questions that might be presented to you on a quiz, a test, or an exam will be seen as a variation of these problems or a change of the numbers within the problems.

Your confidence in the material will grow over time, and your ability to write tests will improve vastly. A little effort is involved in answering the questions for each chapter, but once done, you will see similar phrases in other questions, similar mathematical components needed, and you will be able to find the required answers to the questions that are posed to you.

It is imperative that you attempt each question prior to looking at the answers. There is a vast difference between seeing how a question is done and actually doing a question. When you look at an answer, the wording, the graph, or the mathematics, you can follow along, and it will make sense; however, reproducing a similar answer on an exam is vastly different. Can you remember the labelling of the graph? Which curves should appear on which graph? What causes the shifts of those curves? In which direction should those shifts move? If price changes, do you shift the curve or merely move along the curve? Only when you do these questions and do them prior to looking at the answers will you be able to first understand where in a particular problem you are having difficulties and where in a given chapter you are struggling.

Trying a problem, drawing a graph, and attempting the mathematics are all part of the process of learning. You do learn and retain that knowledge if you work a problem through and you draw the graphs. There is something to be said for the old adage, 'Practice makes perfect'. One of the best ways to study for an economics test is to redo the problems and draw the graphs.

Much of the work that we do in economics is cumulative. To be able to understand this week's material you have to make an effort to learn last week's material. The easiest way to do this is to adopt a weekly work plan.

As my good friend, Professor Soroka would always tell his classes:
> *Go to lectures. It is easier to learn when you hear explanations, write notes and construct diagrams step-by-step. Each week, do the assigned problems, as well as some multiple-choice questions. Answering the problems and multiple-choice questions helps you to learn, and to find out if you understand the course material. Attend tutorials. Solve problems, review difficult material and ask questions about anything you do not understand. Above all, do not get discouraged.*

This workbook is not meant to supplant either the text or study guide, but rather to be used in conjunction with them to assist you in understanding the material and increasing your chances of success. I hope you find economic as much fun as I do. Enjoy learning!

Marilyn Cottrell

1. Inflation Rate $= \dfrac{P_2 - P_1}{P_1} \times 100\%$ $P_2 =$ New CPI
   $P_1 =$ PREVIOUS

2. Unemployment Rate $= \dfrac{\text{\# of people unemployed}}{\text{The labour force}} \times 100$ labour force $=$ # of people employed
   $+$
   # of people unemployed

PART SEVEN
AN INTRODUCTION TO MACROECONOMICS

3. The real interest $=$ The nominal interest Rate $-$ the Rate of Inflation.

Tutorial #1
Chapter 19: *What Macroeconomics Is All About*

4. CPI $= \dfrac{\text{Current Pricelevel}}{\text{Base Period price level}} \times 100$

It is imperative that you make an effort to attempt all the questions.

Assignment #1: Key Macroeconomics Variables

Multiple Choice:
Questions similar to the following are asked in a multiple-choice format. Rather than taking a guess, try to answer each of the following questions.

1. The Consumer Price Index (CPI) for September of 2004 was 125; however, in September of 2005 the CPI was given as 128. What was the annual rate of inflation during this period? (1992 = 100)

   Rate of inflation $= \dfrac{\text{CPI year 2005} - \text{CPI year 2004}}{\text{CPI year 2004}} \times 100 = \dfrac{128-125}{125}$
   $= \dfrac{3}{125} \times 100$
   $= 2.4\%$

2. In September 2005, the population of Canada was approximately 32 million. There were 16.2 million persons employed and 1.1 million persons unemployed. Statistics Canada requests that you find the September 2005 unemployment rate.

   Unemployment Rate $= \dfrac{1.1}{16.2+1.1} \times 100 = \dfrac{1.1}{17.3} \times 100 = 6.36\%$ $\dfrac{\text{No. of unemployed}}{\text{No. of labour force}}$

3. The Consumer Price Index (CPI) for the month of August 2005 was 128 and the CPI for the month of July 2005 was given as 127.5. What is your estimate of the average annual rate of inflation for 2005? (1992 = 100)

   $\dfrac{128-127.5}{127.5} \times 100 \cdot 12 = 4.71\%$

4. Find the real interest rate when the nominal interest rate is given as 8% and inflation is running at 3%.

   Real interest rate $=$ nominal interest rate $-$ inflaction rate
   $= 8\% - 3\%$
   $= 5\%$

True/False:
For the next two questions, indicate whether the statements are true or false, and briefly explain your answer. You may use a fully labeled diagram to support your explanation. (These true/false questions could also be posed as discussion questions.)

1. If more people are employed, the unemployment rate must go down.
   False. This is because labour force are increasing $\Rightarrow$ number of employed and number of unemployment are increasing. $\therefore$ Unemployment rate may not go down.

2. The Consumer Price Index (CPI) underestimates the increase in the cost of living.
   过低的评价
   False.
   CPI $\Rightarrow$ lower #.
   CPI look at average of services (quantitty).
   ~~keep the fri~~ Price change.

CPI keep the basket of good. (keep the quality)

Base year CPI = 100.
CPI is buyer.
① has fixed way for buyer,
when the base year change, Price will change

CPI $\Rightarrow$ Quantity/ price
keep quality.

1

Problems:

1. The following table shows the goods and services consumed by a typical urban household in the economy of Niagara-on-the-Vine. (You are calculating the fixed, base-weighted Consumer Price Index.)

(handwritten, left margin)

b)
$$CPI_t = \frac{\Sigma P_t Q_o}{\Sigma P_o Q_o} \times 100$$

Price in current year ↑

Price in the base year ↓

$= \frac{3390}{2770} \times 100$

≈ 122.38

Good	Quantity in Base Basket	Base Period Price	Expenditure	Current Period Price	Expenditure
Grapes	600 baskets	$2.20	$1320	$2.40	$1440
Ice wine chocolates	300 each	$2.50	$750	$3.00	900
Wine tasting	700 each	$1.00	$700	$1.50	1050
			$2770		$3390

a) Fill in the preceding table.
b) Calculate the Consumer Price Index for the current period.
c) Find the rate of inflation between the base period and the current period.
d) Has there been a change in the relative prices of goods?

(handwritten, left margin)

c)
Rate of Inflation $= \frac{CPI_{now} - CPI_{before}}{CPI_{before}} \times 100$

$= \frac{3390 - 2770}{2770} \times 100$

$\approx 22.38\%$

or

C. inflation Rate

$= \frac{122.38 - 100}{100} \times 100\%$

$= 22.38\%$

(handwritten, under d)
Grapes : (2.40-2.20)/2.20 × 100 = 9.09%
IWC : (3-2.5)/2.5 × 100 = 20%
Wine tasting : (1.5-1)/1 × 100 = 50%

2. Canadian implicit price index [Gross Domestic Product (GDP) at market prices] with the base year, 1997 = 100.

Year	Index
1992	92.7
1993	94.0
1994	95.1
1995	97.2
1996	98.8
1997	100.0
1998	99.6
1999	101.3
2000	105.5
2001	106.7
2002	107.8
2003	111.2
2004	114.8

(handwritten)
a) 2000 = 105.5   2001 = 106.7
Rate of annual inflation $= \frac{106.7 - 105.5}{105.5} \times 100\% = 1.14\%$

b) 2002 = 107.8   2003 = 111.2
Rate of annual inflation $= \frac{111.2 - 107.8}{107.8} \times 100\% = 3.15\%$

c) base year = 100   (1997 = 100)   2004 = 114.8
Rate of inflation $= \frac{114.8 - 100}{100} \times 100\% = 14.8\%$

a) Calculate the annual inflation rate from 2000 to 2001.
b) Calculate the annual inflation rate from 2002 to 2003.
c) What was the rate of inflation from the base year to 2004?

*Note: State your answers correct to two decimal places.
Answers: Page 31.

Tutorial #2

Chapter 20: *The Measurement of National Income and Product*

Assignment #2: National Income Accounting

Multiple Choice:
Choose the one alternative that best completes the statement or answers the question.

1. The definition of gross domestic product is as follows:
   a) the final value of all goods that are produced in the economy in a given time period.
   b) the market value of all goods and services that are produced in the economy during a given time period.
   c) the total market value of all goods and services produced in the economy during a given time period.
   d) the average value of all output produced in the economy in a given time period.
   e) the total market value of all the intermediate goods and services that are produced in the economy for a given time period.

*Note: At times there may appear to be more than one correct answer; however, only one will be a definition.

2. Which one of the following is **not** true?
   a) $Y = C + I + G + IM - X$ $GDP = C + I + G + X - IM$
   b) $I + [X - IM] = S + [T - G] \rightarrow$ National saving $\left.\begin{array}{l} \text{National saving} \\ \text{National assets} \end{array}\right\}$ the same.
   c) $Y = C + S + T$ $\longrightarrow$
   d) $Y + IM = C + I + G + X$
   e) $Y = C + I + G + NX$

*Note: Four out of five answers are correct, and you must remember to find the wrong answer.

Questions similar to the following are asked in a multiple-choice format. Rather than taking a guess, try to answer each of the following questions.

3. The Gross Domestic Product (GDP) for the month July 2005 is given as $1070 billion. Statistics Canada tells us that the GDP for July 2005 is an increase of 2.6% over the GDP for July 2004. Please find the value of the July 2004 GDP. (1997 chained $)

$$\frac{1070 - P_1}{P_1} \times 100 = 2.6\%$$

$$1070 - P_1 = 0.026 P_1$$

$$1.026 P_1 = 1070$$

$$P_1 = 1042.88$$

$$\approx 1043.$$

a) the change in production $= \Delta$ In real GDP.

$= 278045 - 267884$

$= 10161$

GDP deflator $= \dfrac{\text{Nominal GDP}}{\text{real GDP}} \times 100.$

Nominal $- 028 \Delta P$

Real $= \Delta P.$

(4.) Canadian real GDP (Y) for the first quarter of 2004 was given as $267,884 billion, whereas the real GDP for the first quarter of 2005 was given as $278,045 billion. Nominal GDP for the first quarter of 2004 was $301,137 billion, and the nominal GDP for the first quarter of 2005 was $319,833.

a) What is the value of the change in production? $\quad 278045 - 267884 = 10161$

b) State the growth rate of real GDP. $\quad \dfrac{10161}{267884} \times 100 = 3.79\%$

c) What is the value of the GDP deflator for the first quarter of 2004? In 2005?

d) State the inflation rate between the first quarter of 2005 and the first quarter of 2004 using the GDP deflator.

C) 2004:

$\dfrac{301137}{267884} \times 100$

$= 112.41$

2005: $\dfrac{319833}{278045} \times 100$

$= 115.03$

d) $\dfrac{115.03 - 112.41}{112.41} \times 100 = 2.33\%$

True/False:

For the next two questions, indicate whether the statement is true or false and briefly explain your answer. You may use a fully labeled diagram to enhance your answer if you wish.

1. The change in Capital Stock is positive if Gross Investment is increasing. False. Gross investment = Net Investment + Depreciation ⌐ both have to increase.

2. Gross domestic income at factor cost includes wages and salaries plus interest plus business profits plus depreciation plus indirect taxes minus subsidies. ~~at market price~~ False. If it said at the market price it will be Ture.

Problems:

1. You are given the following information about the economy of Moose Bottom (all figures are in millions of dollars):

Consumption = $200

Savings = $275

Net investment = $70

Transfer payments = $90

Subsidies = $10

Taxes = $25

Government expenditures = $100
(purchases)

Depreciation = $30

Exports = $150

Wages and salaries = $300

Imports = $50

Interest = $50

C) $I + [X - IM]$
$\dfrac{}{4}$

d) $S + [T - G]$
$\dfrac{}{4}$

a) What is the value of real GDP in Moose Bottom?

$Y = C + I + G + X - IM$
$= 200 + (70 + 30) + 100 + 150 - 50$
$= 500$

b) State the value of net domestic income at factor costs in the economy of Moose Bottom.

$GDP = GDI \text{ at market price}. \quad NDI = GDI - Depreciation - Taxes + Subsides.$
$= 500 - 30 - 25 + 10 = 455.$

c) What is the value of national asset formation?

d) What is the value of national savings?

e) What relationship have you discovered between part (b), the value of national asset formation, and part (c), the value of national savings?

C) National asset Formation = Gross Investment + Net exports
$= (70 + 30 \text{ Net}) + (150 - 50)$
$= 200$

d) National savings = Saving + (Taxes - Government expenditure) $= 275 + (25 \bar{0} 100)$
$= 200$

e). the relationship between these two are always equal. Both are 200

4

2. Following is the data for the economy of Bella Venezia, where there are three final goods and services produced: Pizza, Vino (Wine), and Gondola Rides.

	Current Year Output	Price	Current Period Expenditure	Price	Base Period Expenditure
Pizza (each)	10,000	$10	$100000	$8	$80000
Vino (Wine) (bottles)	6,000	$30	180000	$25	150 000
Gondola Rides (each)	5,000	$50	250000	$40	200 000
Total Expenditure			$530000		430000

a) Calculate the total expenditures for this economy at both base and current year prices.
b) What is the value of nominal GDP in the current period? $530000 0
c) What is the value of real GDP in the current period? $ 430000
d) What is the GDP deflator in the current period?

$$GDP\ deflator = \frac{Current}{base} \times 100 = \frac{530000}{430000} \times 100$$

$$= 123.26$$

inflation rate is 23.26.

3. You are given the following information about the economy of Mystery Heights (all figures are in billions of dollars):

Consumption = $4190
Interest = $300
Net investment = $1125
Imports = $495   purchases
Government expenditures = $1250
Indirect taxes = $165

Depreciation = $175
Exports = $485
Wages and salaries = $5,500
Subsidies = $35
Business profits = $625

Gross Investment = Net Investment + Deprecation

a) GDP = C+I+G+X-IM = 4190+1125+1250+485 - 495 +175 = 6730

a) Find the value of real gross domestic product at market prices.
b) Find the value of gross domestic income at market prices.
c) What is the value of net domestic income at factor cost?

Answers: Page 35.

b) GDP=GDI ∴ GDI=6730

c) NDI = GDI - Depreciation - Taxes + Subsides
= 6730 - 175 - 165 + 35
= 6425

NDI = wages and salaries + Business profits + Interest
= 5500 + 625 + 300
= 6425   (factor cost)

5

Tutorial - 02

1. GDP From the expenditure side:

$$Y = GDP = C + \underset{\downarrow}{I} + G + \underbrace{X - IM}_{\longrightarrow Nx \,(Net\ exports)}$$

Gross Investment = Net Investment + Depreciation.

2. GDP from Income side:

GDP = GDI at Market Price = Factor Incomes + Non-factor Payments

$\Rightarrow$ GDI = $\underline{(Salaries\ \&\ wages + Interest + Business\ Profits)}$

Factor incomes $\Rightarrow$ NDI

+ Indirect Taxes + Depreciation − Subsidies.

3. GDP Deflator

$$GDP\ Deflator = \frac{GDP\ at\ current\ Price}{GDP\ at\ real\ price} \times 100$$

$$= \frac{Nominal\ GDP}{real\ GDP} \times 100$$

Tutorial #3
Chapter 21: *The Simplest Short-Run Macro Model*

Assignment #3: Desired Aggregate Expenditure
(total spending)

Multiple Choice:
Choose the one alternative that best completes the statement or answers the question.

e

1. In general, the consumption function shows that as disposable income increases, consumption
    a) falls and savings rise.
    b) and savings are both constant.
    c) is constant and savings fall.
    d) is constant and savings rise.
    e) and savings will both rise.

5,000

2. If a typical household's disposable income rose from $45,000 to $50,000 and their desired consumption expenditures also rose from $27,000 to $29,800, we can conclude that
    2,800
    a) marginal propensity to save is 0.56.
    b) average propensity to save is 0.56.
    Saving ↑ 2,200
    e
    c) marginal propensity to consume is $2,800.
    $\frac{2800}{500}$
    d) average propensity to consume is 0.56.
    $\frac{2800}{5000} = 0.56$
    e) marginal propensity to consume is 0.56.

3. Savings is measured as disposable income minus
    a) net taxes.   *Disposable income − Consumption expenditure*
    b) net taxes plus subsidies.
    d
    c) average savings.   *=Saving*
    d) consumption expenditure.
    e) transfer payments.

4. Disposable income is   *$Y_D = C + S$*
    a) equal to consumption minus savings.
    b
    b) equal to consumption expenditures plus savings.
    c) equal to real gross domestic product minus consumption.
    d) equal to real gross domestic product plus savings.
    e) equal to real gross domestic product minus transfer payments.

5. The marginal propensity to consume is calculated as $MPC = \frac{\Delta C}{\Delta Y}$

   a) total consumption divided by the change in disposable income.
   b) total consumption divided by the change in real gross domestic product.
   c) the change in total consumption divided by the change in total disposable income.
   d) the change in marginal consumption divided by the change in total disposable income.
   e) total consumption divided by total disposable income.

6. If the consumption function lies above the 45-degree reference line, households
   a) are dissaving.
   b) are consuming all their disposable income.
   c) are saving more than they are consuming.
   d) are saving all their disposable income.
   e) are consuming more than they are saving.

7. The multiplier process describes changes that occur in
   a) autonomous expenditure brought about by a change in income.
   b) induced expenditure brought about by a change in disposable income.
   c) the equilibrium level of income caused by changes in autonomous expenditure.
   d) investment expenditure brought about by a change in real gross domestic product.
   e) autonomous expenditure brought about by changes in the price level.

True/False:
For the next two questions, indicate whether the statement is true or false and briefly explain your answer. You may use a fully labeled diagram to enhance your answer if you wish.

$Y_D = C + S$ $Y_D = Y - T$

1. Disposable income is the income that households have left after paying for basic expenses such as food and housing.

2. Real gross domestic product is equal to consumption expenditures plus savings. plus net taxes

$Y = C + S + T$

$$Y = \underbrace{C + S}_{} + T$$

$$Y_D.$$

8

Problems:

1. Welcome to the economy of Spend-it-up Village. Given in the following schedule is disposable income and consumption for this economy.

disposable income   *consumption*   *saving*

$\Delta Yd = 500$ $\Delta C = 450$ $\Delta S = 50$ $Yd = C + S$

Yd is income − taxes
= I − T

Yd	C	S
0	100	−100
500	550	−50
1000	1000	0
1500	1450	50
2000	1900	100
2500	2350	150
3000	2800	200

a) From this information, fill in the column for savings.   *marginal propensity to saving = 0.1*

b) State the value of the marginal propensity to consume out of disposable income. $MPC_{Yd} = \frac{\Delta C}{\Delta Yd} = \frac{450}{500} = 0.9$ *(extra)*

c) What is the value of the autonomous component of consumption? *when Yd = 0, then C = 100*

d) Write the consumption function. $C = a + bYd$ $C = 100 + 0.9Yd$

e) State the value of the marginal propensity to save out of disposable income. $MPS_{Yd} = \frac{\Delta S}{\Delta Yd} = \frac{50}{500} = 0.1$

f) What is the value of the autonomous component of savings? *when Yd = 0, S = −100*

g) Write the savings function. $S = -100 + 0.1Yd$ $S = -a + (1-b)Yd$

h) What are the similarities between these two functions?

$S + C = 1$

inversity

$Y_D = C + S$

$mpc + mps = 1$

$Y_D = (a_c + mpc \cdot Y_D) + (-a_c + mps \cdot Y_D)$

2. In the economy of Badgerville, the simplified aggregate expenditure function $(AE = C + I)$ is given as:

$$AE = 250 + 0.6Y$$

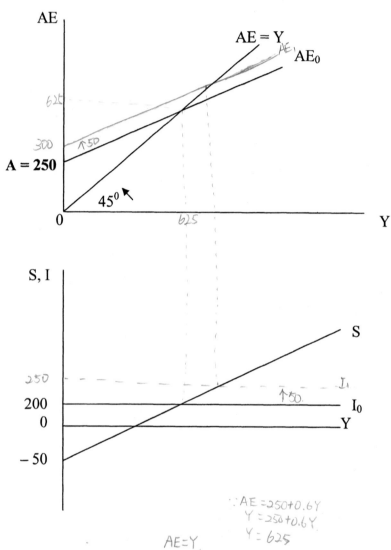

a) Find the <u>equilibrium level of real GDP.</u>
b) Show this level of real gross domestic product on both of the preceding graphs.
c) State the value of the <u>simple multiplier</u>. $K = \frac{1}{1-z} = \frac{1}{1-0.6} = 2.5$
d) If investment increases by 50, what is the change in real GDP that will result? $K = \frac{\Delta Y}{\Delta I}$ $\Delta Y = K \cdot \Delta I$
$= 2.5 \times 50$
$= 125$
e) Show the change in investment and the change in aggregate expenditures on the preceding diagrams.
f) What is the value of the marginal propensity to save?
Answers: Page 41.

$MPC = 0.6$ $MPS = 0.4$

[handwritten top:] $AE = C + I$ ↳ autonomous.

[handwritten right:] as $MPM \uparrow \to K \downarrow$.
as $t \uparrow \to K \downarrow$

Tutorial #4
Chapter 22: *Adding Government and Trade to the Simple Macro Model*

[handwritten:] $C = a + MPC \cdot Y_D$

Assignment #4: Introducing Government and Trade

[handwritten:] $AE = C + I + G + N_X.$ *auto auto* $N_X = X - IM$ *auto i.e.*

Multiple Choice:
Choose the one alternative that best completes the statement or answers the question.

[handwritten:] change in income

1. The presence of induced taxes means
   a) fiscal policy multipliers are made larger.
   b) discretionary fiscal policy is weakened.
   c) there is always a deficit. *[handwritten:]* ↳ only taxes, we can not effect fiscal policy.
   d) there are no transfer payments.
   e) fluctuations in aggregate expenditure are reduced.

[handwritten right:] $I \uparrow \Rightarrow Tax \uparrow$.
Disposable I ↓ ⟹ Consume ↓
Government use tax to effect economic
When we have tax, $k = \frac{1}{1-z}$ be can smaller.
$k = \frac{1}{1-z}$ (no government & no trade) close economy

2. A rise in the domestic price level will
   a) increase the level of desired aggregate expenditures.
   b) decrease desired aggregate expenditures only if household incomes change.
   c) cause net exports to rise.
   d) decrease desired aggregate expenditures because the real value of wealth would change.
   e) have no effect on the level of desired aggregate expenditures.

[handwritten:] $P \uparrow$ AED open economy: gov/trade $z = MPC(1-t) - m$ net import ppl spending tax

3. Assuming a constant price level, an increase in autonomous expenditures will cause the AE curve to shift
   a) upward and the aggregate demand curve shifts leftward.
   b) downward and a movement rightward along the aggregate demand curve.
   c) downward and the aggregate demand curve shifts leftward.
   d) upward and the aggregate demand curve shifts rightward.
   e) downward and the aggregate demand curve shifts rightward.

[handwritten:] $a \uparrow$ $AE \uparrow$ $b \uparrow$ $AE = a + bY$

[handwritten:] build in
4. The automatic fiscal stabilizers that affect aggregate expenditures are
   a) autonomous taxation.
   b) progressive income taxes and employment insurance payments.
   c) government purchases of goods and services. *[handwritten:]* ↳ Close to the consumption.
   d) interest rates and exchange rates.
   e) the marginal propensity to consume.

5. The autonomous tax multiplier
   a) has the same value as the government expenditures multiplier during recessions and inflations.
   b) is smaller than the government expenditures multiplier. *[handwritten:]* $k = \frac{1}{1-z}$ $K_t = \frac{-MPC}{1-z}$ $k = \frac{1}{1-z}$
   c) is larger than the government expenditures multiplier.
   d) is larger than the government expenditures multiplier at potential GDP.
   e) and the government expenditures multiplier are always equal.

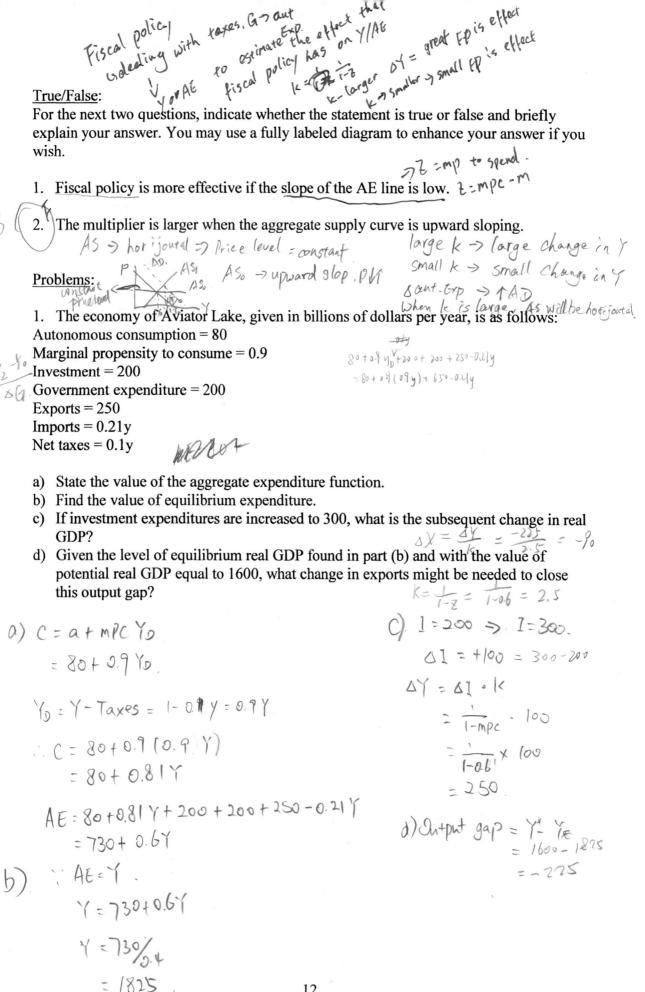

Fiscal policy
udealing with taxes, G→ aut
to estimate the effect that
fiscal policy has on Y/AE
$k = \frac{1}{1-z}$
k larger, ΔY = great FP is effect
k→smaller → small FP is effect

True/False:

For the next two questions, indicate whether the statement is true or false and briefly explain your answer. You may use a fully labeled diagram to enhance your answer if you wish.

→z = mp to spend.

1. Fiscal policy is more effective if the <u>slope of the AE line is low.</u> $z = mpc - m$

always
on the
exam

2. The multiplier is larger when the aggregate supply curve is upward sloping.

$AS \to$ horizontal $\Rightarrow$ Price level = constant

$AS_0 \to$ upward slop, P↑↓

large k → large change in Y
small k → small change in Y
δ aut. Exp $\to \uparrow AD$
When k is large, AS will be horizontal.

$k = \frac{Y_1 - Y_0}{\delta G}$

$\to k = \frac{Y_2 - Y_0}{\delta G}$

Problems:

1. The economy of Aviator Lake, given in billions of dollars per year, is as follows:
   - Autonomous consumption = 80
   - Marginal propensity to consume = 0.9
   - Investment = 200
   - Government expenditure = 200
   - Exports = 250
   - Imports = 0.21y
   - Net taxes = 0.1y

$80 + 0.9 y_D^V + 200 + 200 + 250 - 0.21y$
$= 80 + 0.9(0.9y) + 650 - 0.21y$

   a) State the value of the aggregate expenditure function.
   b) Find the value of equilibrium expenditure.
   c) If investment expenditures are increased to 300, what is the subsequent change in real GDP?

   $\Delta Y = \frac{\Delta Y}{k} = \frac{-225}{2.5} = -90$

   d) Given the level of equilibrium real GDP found in part (b) and with the value of potential real GDP equal to 1600, what change in exports might be needed to close this output gap?

   $k = \frac{1}{1-z} = \frac{1}{1-0.6} = 2.5$

a) $C = a + mPC \, Y_D$

   $= 80 + 0.9 \, Y_D$

   $Y_D = Y - Taxes = 1 - 0.1 \, y = 0.9 \, Y$

   $\therefore C = 80 + 0.9(0.9 \, Y)$
   $= 80 + 0.81 \, Y$

   $AE = 80 + 0.81 \, Y + 200 + 200 + 250 - 0.21 \, Y$
   $= 730 + 0.6 \, Y$

b) $\because AE = Y$.

   $Y = 730 + 0.6 \, Y$

   $Y = \frac{730}{0.4}$

   $= 1825$.

c) $I = 200 \Rightarrow I = 300$.

   $\Delta I = +100 = 300 - 200$

   $\Delta Y = \Delta I \cdot k$
   $= \frac{1}{1-mpc} \cdot 100$
   $= \frac{1}{1-0.6} \times 100$
   $= 250$.

d) Output gap $= Y^* - Y_E$
   $= 1600 - 1825$
   $= -225$

12

e) On the aggregate demand and aggregate supply diagram and also on the aggregate expenditure diagram, draw the original or beginning position of the price level, real GDP, and state the value of autonomous expenditures.

Desired AE

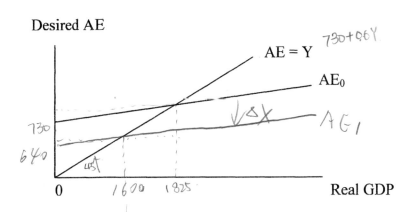

Price Level

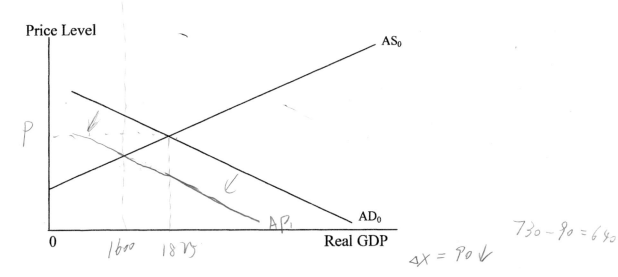

$730 - 90 = 640$

$\Delta X = 90$ ↓

f) On the aggregate demand and aggregate supply diagram and also on the aggregate expenditure diagram show the changes that result from a change in exports.
g) Show the decrease in the price level on the aggregate expenditure graph.
h) If government expenditures remained at $200 and autonomous taxes were increased by $100, what change would result in real GDP?
i) The tax multiplier is given by $K_T = \dfrac{-b}{1-z}$.

   Why is $-b$ used in the numerator?
j) State the formula for the transfer payments multiplier.

13

2. The following schedule relates to the economy of Carnival Bay (in billions of dollars).

Y	C	+	I	+	G	+	X	−	IM	AE
0	50		50		60		60		0	220
100	110		50		60		60		15	265
200	170		50		60		60		30	310
300	230		50		60		60		45	355
400	290		50		60		60		60	400
500	350		50		60		60		75	445
600	410		50		60		60		90	490

a) Fill in the preceding chart.
b) State the value of autonomous expenditure. $Y=0$ $A=220$
c) State the value of the marginal propensity to consume out of real GDP. $MPC = \frac{\Delta C}{\Delta Y} = \frac{60}{100} = 0.6$
d) When real GDP is equal to 200, what is the value of aggregate expenditures? 310
e) Discuss the situation that exists at this level with respect to inventories and the ensuing production decisions. $Y=200$ $AE=310$ Y (producing). $Y-AE=200-310 = -110$ AE (selling). Economic should increase production.
f) When real GDP is equal to 500, what is the value of aggregate expenditure? 445
g) Discuss the situation that exists at this new level with respect to inventories and the ensuing production decisions. producing > selling. Economic should decrease production
h) State the value of the marginal propensity to import. $MPM = \frac{\Delta IM}{\Delta Y} = \frac{15}{100} = 0.15$
i) Find the slope of the aggregate expenditure [AE] equation, which is the marginal propensity to spend [z]. $z = \frac{\Delta AE}{\Delta Y} = \frac{45}{100} = 0.45$
j) Find the value of the simple fixed-price multiplier. $k = \frac{1}{1-z} = \frac{1}{1-0.45} = 1.82$
Answers: Page 47.

14

Tutorial #5
Chapter 23: *Output and Prices in the Short Run* **and Chapter 24:** *Output and Prices in the Long Run*

Assignment #5: Aggregate Demand, Aggregate Supply, and the Price Level
This assignment runs over two weeks.

Multiple Choice:
Choose the one alternative that best completes the statement or answers the question.

1. Which of the following does **not** affect aggregate demand?
   a) changes in expected future income
   b) changes in fiscal policy
   c) changes in monetary policy
   d) changes in technological change
   e) changes in the exchange rate

2. Ceteris paribus, all else remaining the same, potential GDP increases with a(n)
   a) decrease in the labour force.
   b) advance in technology.
   c) decrease in capital stock.
   d) fall in wages.
   e) drop in the price level.

3. An output gap occurs in the economy when
   a) nominal GDP is greater than the real GDP.
   b) demand for labour is high.
   c) actual GDP and potential GDP differ.
   d) potential national income is greater than equilibrium national income.
   e) actual GDP equals potential GDP.

True/False:
For the next two questions, indicate whether the statement is true or false and briefly explain your answer. You may use a fully labeled diagram to enhance your answer if you wish.

1. If government expenditures are increased in an economy that is presently in long-run equilibrium, the resulting change in real gross domestic product will be permanent.

2. Fiscal policy provides a speedier recovery from a recession than does the self-adjustment mechanism.

↑G → ↑AD → ↑Y

Y > Y* ⇒ inflationary gap

↑W → ↑ unit cost → AS shifts left

→ ↑P → Y move to potential

2. Fiscal Policy:
↑G or ↓T ⇒ ↑AD   ↑Y
The S-adj:
↓W → ↑AS, ↑Y takes a long time for W to decline
∴ Fiscal policy is a speeder Solution

Problems:

Price Level

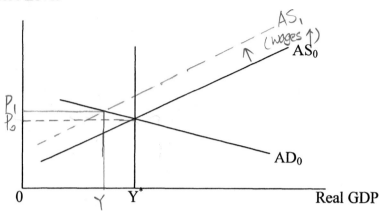

1. The economy of Snowtown is initially in long-run equilibrium. Please analyze the following actions on the price level and real GDP as the economy moves to a new equilibrium position. Explain both graphically and verbally.
   (Hint: Draw a new diagram for each example.)

   stagflation.

   a) The nominal wage rate increases in Snowtown. W↑ ⇒ AS shift left ⇒ ⊉ Rea GDP ↓
   b) The United States purchases less Snowtown goods. ⊃ ↓ ⇒ Real GDP ↓.
   c) Government expenditures in Snowtown increase. RG↑ ⇒ Real GDP↑
   d) Snowtown productivity increases. ⇒

Price Level

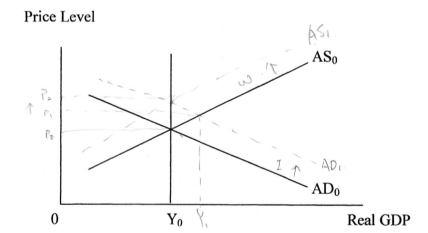

2. Preceding is the economy of Springtime.
   a) Describe the state of the economy of Springtime as depicted in the preceding graph. *long run equilibrium (full employment)*
   b) If investment increased in this economy, label the new price level P_1 and the new real GDP Y_1. Is the economy stable at this new equilibrium level? Explain.
   inflationary gap; not stable (a boom) unemployment < natural rate.

16

c) After the change in investment, if the economy were left to its own devices *w↑* without interference from the government or the Central Bank of Springtime, at *P↑* the new price, P_1, and new real GDP, Y_1, what would you expect to happen? *real GDP > Potential GDP* Explain. *inflationary gap*

Price Level

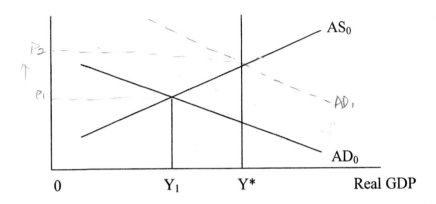

P_2 ↑
P_1
AS_0
AD_1
AD_0

0   Y_1 Y^* Real GDP

real GDP < Potential GDP
recessionary gap

3. Preceding is the economy of Sorokaville.
   a) Describe the state of the economy of Sorokaville as depicted in the preceding graph. *recessionary gap. real GDP < Potential GDP*
   b) If government expenditures increased (to close the output gap) in this economy, *G↑ Tax↓* label the new price level P_2 and the new Real GDP Y_2. Is the economy stable at *⇓ AD↑* this new equilibrium level? Explain. *If Government purchases ↑ to bring economy back to y*↘*
   c) If the economy was still at Y_1 and did not experience interference from the *stable economy* government or the Central Bank of Sorokaville, what would you expect to *⇒ expansionary* happen? Explain. *fiscal policy*

Answers: Page 55. *Y<y* → recessionary gap ⇒ Unempl. < national rate*
the economy is sluggish

SR AS↑, shifts rightward
y↑ back to y ; P↓*

PART NINE
MONEY, BANKING, AND MONETARY POLICY

Tutorial #6
Chapter 27: *The Nature of Money*

Assignment #6: The Canadian Banking System

Multiple Choice:
Choose the one alternative that best completes the statement or answers the question.

1. Fiat money is
   a) backed by gold.
   b) linked to the consumer price index.
   c) money that is decreed to be money by the government.
   d) money used only to pay government employees.
   e) not liquid.
   f) money given out by the car dealer, Fiat.

2. Which one of the following is the most widely accepted form of money?
   a) cheques, credit cards and debit cards
   b) cheques and debit cards
   c) fiat money and cheques
   d) fiat money and debit cards
   e) fiat money

True/False:
For the next question, indicate whether the statement is true or false and briefly explain your answer. You may use a fully labeled diagram to enhance your answer if you wish.
1. An increase in the desired reserve ratio allows for greater money creation in the economy. $\sqrt{} \cdot DM = \frac{1}{\sqrt{} \cdot r}$ the money creation is less

Problems:
1. Pretty Polly Paul, a space cadet from Neptune and a cousin of Miss Tutu from Venus, immigrates to the country of New Canada. She brings along her life savings of $5,000. She deposits this money into the First National Bank of New Canada. The reserve ratio is 10%, and there is no cash drain.
   a) State the deposits multiplier. $DM = \frac{1}{\sqrt{}} = \frac{1}{10\%} = 10$ $DM = \frac{1}{\sqrt{}} = \frac{1}{0.1} = 10$.
   b) Fill in the following T-account showing the initial effects on the First National Bank of New Canada.

bank run
reserve ratio

19

First National Bank of New Canada

Assets		Liabilities	
Reserves	+ 500	Demand Deposits +5000	
Loans	+ 4500		
Total	+ 5000	Total	+5000.

c) Is this money creation or money destruction? *money creation* (*New money coming*)

d) In the following T-account, show the effect on the <u>entire banking system</u> in New Canada.

$$DM = \frac{1}{r} = \frac{1}{0.1} = 10.$$

$$5000 \times 10 = 50000$$

All Banks in New Canada

Assets		Liabilities	
Reserves	+ 5000	Deposits	+ 50000
Loans	+ 45000		
Total	+ 50000	Total	+ 500.00

e) State the total change in <u>reserves.</u> Initial (reserves = +500 x10 =5000   R . DM = ΔR.

f) What is the overall change in <u>loans?</u> Initial loan =+4500 *10 =45000   L . DM = ΔL

g) State the total change in <u>deposits.</u> +5000 x10 =50000

h) What is the total change in the money supply? Has the money supply increased or decreased?

ΔMS = DM × ΔD ← change deposit

= 10 × 5000 = 50000

money supply is money available in the market.

2. Prior to Ms. Paul entering the economy of New Canada, The First National Bank of New Canada had been a Monopoly bank, and its existing <u>deposits were $3,000.</u> It also had existing reserves of <u>$300,</u> and the bank was fully loaned out—<u>no excess reserves.</u>

Monopoly Bank of New Canada

Assets		Liabilities	
Reserves	+ 300	Demand Deposits	+ 3000
Loans	+ 2700		
Total	+ 3000	Total	+3000

What was the final change in the banking system in New Canada after Ms. Paul's deposit of $5,000? [10% target reserves]

Monopoly Bank of New Canada

Assets		$^{\prime 0.1}$	Liabilities	
Reserves	+ 5300		Deposits + 53000	
Loans	+ 47700			
Total	+ 53000		Total	+ 53000

3. Poor Polly Paul is homesick and decides to emigrate from New Canada and travel back to her home planet of Neptune. She finds New Canadians too liberal for her liking. Polly withdraws all her savings, $4,000, ready for her new adventure. The target reserve ratio is now 20%, and there is no cash drain.
   a) What is the value of the deposits multiplier? $DM = \frac{1}{20\%} = 5$
   b) In the following T-account, show the initial result of this withdrawal from the First National Bank of New Canada.

First National Bank of New Canada

Assets		Liabilities	
Reserves	− 800	` Demand Deposits	− 4000
Loans	−3200		
Total	−4000	Total	−4000

   c) Is this money creation or money destruction? Money destruction
   d) State the effect on the entire banking system in New Canada.

All Banks in New Canada

Assets		Liabilities		4000 × 5 = 20000
Reserves	−4000	Deposits	−20000	
Loans	− 16000			
Total	−20000	Total	−20000	

   e) What is the total change in the money supply? Has the money supply increased or decreased?

$$\Delta MS = DM \times \Delta D$$
$$= 5 \times (-4000)$$
$$= -20000. \quad \text{Decrease}$$

$$V = 10\%, \qquad DM = \frac{1}{V} = \frac{1}{0.1} = 10$$

4. Fill in the following chart showing the process of creating money when the desired reserve ratio is 10% and there is no cash drain.

100 × 0.1 = 10   100 − 10 = 90.

Bank	Deposits	=	Reserves	+	Loans
A	$100		10		90
B	90		9		81
C	81		8.1		72.9
	:		:		:
Total	1000		100		900.

↖ Initial Deposit × DM

5. The following shows the balance sheet of The Shady Bank with no excess reserves:

The Shady Bank

$V = 0.1$
$= \frac{100}{1000} = \frac{reserve}{Deposit} = 0.1$

Assets		Liabilities	
Cash/Reserves	$ 100	Deposits	$1,000
Loans	$1,100	Capital	$ 200
Total	$1,200	Total	$1,200

a) The bank now receives a new deposit of $100. Show the position of this bank after it has adjusted to the new deposit (assume no cash drain).

The Shady Bank

Assets		Liabilities	
Cash/Reserves	$ 110	Deposits	$ 1100
Loans	$ 1190	Capital	$ 200
Total	$ 1300	Total	$ 1300

$DM = \frac{1}{0.1} = 10.$ $\Delta D = DM \cdot Deposit.$ $\Delta D = 100 \times 10 = 1000$

b) What is the final increase in bank deposits after the whole process is completed?
c) What would the final increase in deposits be if there was a 10% cash drain?

Answers: Page 63.

$mm = \frac{1}{(c) + V} = \frac{1}{0.1 + 0.1} = \frac{1}{0.2} = 5.$
money multiple

cash drain $mm \cdot \Delta D = 5 \times 100 = 500

$\Delta D \cdot DM = $100 \cdot 10 = 1000

Tutorial #7
Chapter 28: *Money, Interest Rates, and Economic Activity*

Assignment #7: Bonds and the Monetary Transmission Mechanism

Multiple Choice:
Choose the one alternative that best completes the statement or answers the question.

1. If together all the banks in the banking system have $30 million in cash reserves and
    have a desired reserve ratio of 3% percent, the maximum amount of demand deposits
    the banking system can support is
    a) $9 million.
    b) $60 million.
    c) $90 million.
    d) $1 billion.
    e) $900 million.

    [handwritten: $DM = \frac{1}{V} = \frac{1}{0.03} = 33.33$]
    [handwritten: $V = \frac{3}{\%} = 0.03$]
    [handwritten: Demand deposit = DM . Deposit]
    [handwritten: Demand deposit = 30×33.33 = 1000 million = 1 billion]
    [handwritten: $DM = \frac{1}{V} = \frac{1}{0.03} = 33.33$]

2. Bond prices are
    a) directly related to interest rates.
    b) not affected by changes in money demand.
    c) directly related to the change in interest rates.
    d) not affected by changes in the interest rates.
    e) inversely related to interest rates.

    [handwritten: $\uparrow i \rightarrow \downarrow P_B$]

3. If interest rates are expected to fall in the near future, a rational individual would be
    willing to
    a) buy bonds immediately.
    b) buy bonds only if their prices begin to fall.
    c) maintain only their current bond holdings.
    d) place their money into savings and not buy bonds.
    e) sell bonds immediately.

    [handwritten: now interest is high → P_B low]
    [handwritten: → expect to fall (bonds are cheap)]
    [handwritten: P_B is high]
    [handwritten: sell bonds to make profit]

True/False:
For the next two questions, indicate whether the statement is true or false and briefly
explain your answer. You may use a fully labeled diagram to enhance your answer if you
wish.
1. An increase in interest rates with a relatively flat investment demand curve is
    associated with a small increase in investment, aggregate demand and real GDP.
2. When real GDP increases, money demand increases and interest rates decrease.

Problems:
1. The central bank of Aviator Lake decides it wants to increase the money supply.
   a) What might have prompted this decision?
   b) How would the central bank go about doing this?
   c) On the following diagrams, show the process by which the money supply increases.

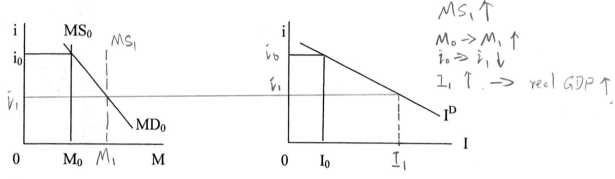

MS, ↑
$M_0 \to M_1$ ↑
$i_0 \to i_1$ ↓
I_1 ↑ → real GDP ↑

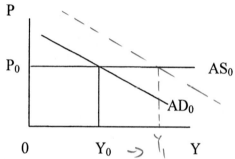

d) Does desired investment expenditure change? Explain.
e) Is the Aviator Lake dollar affected in any way? Explain.
f) Are there any changes in net exports? Explain.
g) Do aggregate demand and real GDP change? Explain.

2. The bank of Aviator Lake decides it wants to decrease the money supply.
   a) What might have prompted this decision?
   b) How would the central bank go about doing this?
   c) On the following diagrams, show the process by which the money supply decreases.

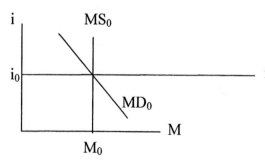

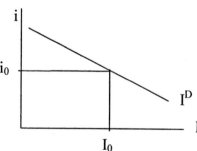

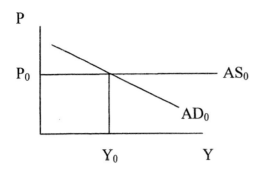

P

P_0 ——————————— AS_0

AD_0

Y_0 Y

d) Does desired investment expenditure change? Explain.
e) Is the Aviator Lake dollar affected in any way? Explain.
f) Are there any changes in net exports? Explain.
g) Do aggregate demand and real GDP change? Explain.

3. The money market is presently not in equilibrium. The interest rates are at a high level. Discuss the relationship between the interest rates and the price of bonds.

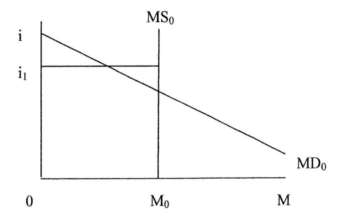

4. The money market is presently not in equilibrium. The interest rates are at a low level. Discuss the relationship between the interest rates and the price of bonds, the need for cash balances, and the opportunity cost for holding money.

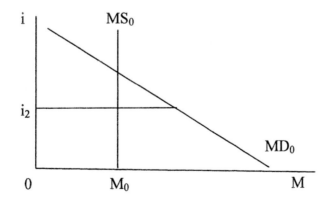

5. Show the monetary transmission mechanism as part of open market operations if the money supply was increased.

6. Using the money-market diagrams, show why monetary policy is more effective with a monetarist approach.

Answers: Page 69.

Tutorial #8
Chapter 29: *Monetary Policy in Canada*

Assignment #8: Open Market Operations, Overnight Loans Rate

Multiple Choice:
Choose the one alternative that best completes the statement or answers the question.

1. Which of the following is *not* one of the four functions of money?
   a) medium of exchange
   b) standard of deferred payment
   c) measure of liquidity
   d) store of value
   e) unit of account

2. A bank can create money by
   a) printing more cheques.
   b) increasing its reserves.
   c) selling some of its bonds.
   d) lending its excess reserves.
   e) converting reserves into bonds.

True/False:
For the next two questions, indicate whether the statement is true or false and briefly explain your answer. You may use a fully labelled diagram to enhance your answer if you wish.
1. If the Bank of Canada wanted to decrease the money supply, it would sell bonds in open market operations.

Discussion Questions:
1. Describe the target that the central bank of Canada (BOC) sets for the overnight interest rate (or, the overnight loans rate).
2. When the BOC sets its target for the overnight interest rate, what other two rates does it set?
3. Why is changing the money supply an ineffective way of conducting monetary policy?
4. State the three reasons why the central bank does not implement policy in this manner.

Problems:

1. In open market operations, the central bank sells $100 million in government bonds.
   a) Do the commercial bank reserves change? If they change, by how much do they change? In which direction would they change?

27

b) If the money multiplier were given as 5, would there be a change in the money supply? If so, by how much would it change? In which direction would it change?
c) Would the interest rates change? (Direction and diagram)
d) Would aggregate demand be affected? Why?
e) Would real GDP change?

2. The central bank buys $100 million in bonds in open market operations. The desired reserves are 10%.
   a) Show the *immediate* effects on the following T-accounts.

Private Households

Assets	Liabilities
Bonds	Deposits

Commercial Banks

Assets	Liabilities
Reserves	Demand Deposits

Central Bank

Assets	Liabilities
Bonds	Commercial bank deposits
	or reserves of commercial banks

   b) What would the commercial banks do now, given that the desired reserves must be addressed?
   c) Do these actions affect the money supply? Explain.

3. Redo the same question as #2; however, all private household funds are now held as deposits in the commercial banks.
   *Note: Only two T-accounts are now used: the T-account for the commercial banks and the T-account for the central bank.

4. With the current interest rate, commercial banks are in need of more cash. There is a growing demand for loans; however, the commercial banks are fully loaned out. The central bank is buying $1,000 in bonds from the commercial banks in open market operations. (Commercial banks are selling bonds.)
   a) Show the *immediate* effects on the T-accounts following.

Commercial Banks

Assets	Liabilities
Reserves	
Bonds	

Central Bank

Assets	Liabilities
Bonds	Currency in circulation

28

b) Discuss the expansion of the money supply that would follow if the target reserve ratio is 10 percent?

c) If all banks in the banking system keep reserves of 10 percent and there is a cash drain of 10 percent, what would be the expected expansion in the money supply?

5. The economy of Aviator Lake is experiencing a recessionary gap. The central bank of Aviator Lake decides to target overnight loans.

   a) How would the central bank of Aviator Lake go about doing this?
   b) On the following diagrams, show the process by which the money market adjusts.

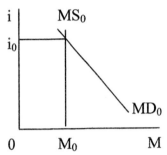

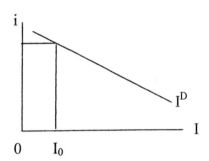

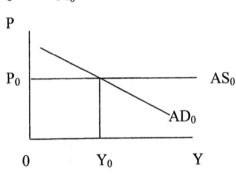

c) Does desired investment expenditure change? Explain.
d) Is the Aviator Lake dollar affected in any way? Explain.
e) Are there any changes in net exports? Explain.
f) Do aggregate demand and real GDP change? Explain.

Answers: Page 77.

Assignment Answers

Assignment #1: Key Macroeconomics Variables

Multiple Choice:

1. The Consumer Price Index (CPI) for September of 2004 was 125; however, in September of 2005 the CPI was given as 128. What was the annual rate of inflation during this period? (1992 = 100)

$$\text{Inflation Rate} = \frac{P_2 - P_1}{P_1} * 100$$

$$= \frac{128 - 125}{125} * 100$$

$$= 2.4\%$$

2. In September 2005, the population of Canada was approximately 32 million. There were 16.2 million persons employed and 1.1 million persons unemployed. Statistics Canada requests that you find the September 2005 unemployment rate.

$$\text{Unemployment Rate} = \frac{\text{\# unemployed}}{\text{Labour force}} * 100$$

$$= \frac{1.1}{16.2 + 1.1} * 100$$

$$= 6.4\%$$

3. The Consumer Price Index (CPI) for the month of August 2005 was 128 and the CPI for the month of July 2005 was given as 127.5. What is your estimate of the average annual rate of inflation for 2005? (1992 = 100)

$$\text{Inflation Rate} = \frac{P_2 - P_1}{P_1} * 100$$

$$= \left[\frac{128 - 127.5}{127.5} * 100 \right] * 12$$

$$= 4.7\%$$

4. Find the real interest rate when the nominal interest rate is given as 8% percent and inflation is running at 3% percent.

$$\text{Real interest rate} = \text{Nominal interest rate} - \text{Inflation}$$

$$\text{Real interest rate} = 8\% \text{ percent} - 3\% \text{ percent}$$

$$\text{Real interest rate} = 5\% \text{ percent}$$

The real interest rate is 5% percent.

True/False:

1. If more people are employed, the unemployment rate must go down.

Because the unemployment rate is a ratio, an increase in employment does **not** necessarily lower unemployment. The labour force may grow, more people are employed, and more may be unemployed.

$$\text{Unemployment rate} = \frac{\text{\# unemployed}}{\text{Labour force}} * 100$$

False

2. The Consumer Price Index (CPI) underestimates the increase in the cost of living.

The CPI overestimates increases in the cost of living because the basket of goods used for the CPI has fixed weights. It tends to overestimate the change in the price level by approximately 0.5% percent per year.
There are built biases within the CPI model.
o Fixed Fixed-weight bias
o New goods bias
o Quality bias
o Outlet substitution
False

Problems:
1. The following table shows the goods and services consumed by a typical household in the economy of Niagara-on-the-Vine. (You are calculating the fixed, base-weighted Consumer Price Index.)

Good	Quantity in Base Basket	Base Period Price	Base Period Expenditure	Current Period Price	Current Period Expenditure
Grapes	600 baskets	$2.20	$1320	$2.40	$1440
Ice wine chocolates	300 each	$2.50	$ 750	$3.00	$ 900
Wine tasting	700 each	$1.00	$ 700	$1.50	$1050
			$2770		$3390

a) Fill in the preceding table stating the value of the base and current year expenditures.

b) Calculate the Consumer Price Index for the current period.

$$\text{CPI}_{\text{current year}} = \frac{\$3390}{\$2770} * 100 = 122.38$$

c) Find the rate of inflation between the base period and the current period.

$$\text{Inflation Rate} = \frac{P_2 - P_1}{P_1} * 100$$

$$= \frac{122.38 - 100}{100} * 100$$

$$= 22.38\%$$

d) Has there been a change in the relative prices of goods?

The price of grapes increased [(2.40 – 2.20) / 2.20] * 100 = 9.09%.
Ice wine chocolates have increased [(3.00 – 2.50) / 2.50] * 100 = 20%.
Wine tasting has increased [(1.50 – 1.00) / 1.00] * 100 = 50%.

*Note: Hints....
1. c) The CPI for the base year is always 100.

$$\text{CPI}_{\text{base year}} = \frac{\$2770}{\$2770} * 100 = 100$$

1. d) Never refer to the inflation rate when discussing relative prices. Relative prices compare the price of one good or service to the price of another good or service.

IPI = GDP at market

2. Canadian implicit price index [Gross Domestic Product (GDP) at market prices] with the base year, 1997 = 100.

1992	92.7
1993	94.0
1994	95.1
1995	97.2
1996	98.8
1997	100.0
1998	99.6
1999	101.3
2000	105.5
2001	106.7
2002	107.8
2003	111.2
2004	114.8

a) Calculate the annual inflation rate from 2000 to 2001.

$$\text{Annual inflation rate} = \frac{106.7 - 105.5}{105.5} * 100$$
$$= 1.14\%$$

b) Calculate the annual inflation rate from 2002 to 2003.

$$\text{Annual inflation rate} = \frac{111.2 - 107.8}{107.8} * 100$$
$$= 3.15\%$$

c) What was the rate of inflation from the base year to 2004? [1997 to 2004]

$$\text{Annual inflation rate} = \frac{114.8 - 100}{100} * 100$$
$$= 14.80\%$$

*Note: State your answers correct to two decimal places.

Assignment #2: National Income Accounting

Multiple Choice:

1. Gross domestic product is defined as   [c]
   a) the final value of all goods produced in the economy in a given time period.
   b) the market value of all goods and services produced in the economy during a given time period.
   c) the total market value of all goods and services produced in the economy during a given time period.
   d) the average value of output produced in the economy in a given time period.
   e) the total market value of all the intermediate goods and services produced in the economy for a given time period.

2. Which one of the following is **not** true?   [a]
   a) $Y = C + I + G + IM - X$ $GDP = C + I + G + X - IM$
   b) $I + [X - IM] = S + [T - G]$
   c) $Y = C + S + T$ $-Import$
   d) $Y + IM = C + I + G + X$ $NX = X - IM$
                                   net export   export
   e) $Y = C + I + G + NX$

3. The Gross Domestic Product (GDP) for the month July 2005 is given as $1070 billion. Statistics Canada tells us that the GDP for July 2005 is an increase of 2.6% over the GDP for July 2004. Please find the value of the July 2004 GDP. (1997 chained $)

Let P_1 represent GDP for July 2004.

$$\frac{1070 - P_1}{P_1} * 100 = 2.6$$

$$\frac{1070 - P_1}{P_1} = \frac{2.6}{100}$$

$$\frac{1070 - P_1}{P_1} = 0.026$$

$$1070 - P_1 = 0.026P_1$$

$$1070 = P_1 + 0.026P_1$$

$$1070 = 1.026P_1$$

$$\frac{1070}{1.026} = P_1$$

$$1042.8849 = P_1$$

$$P_1 = 1043$$

GDP in July 2004 is $1043 billion.

4. Canadian real GDP (Y) for the first quarter of 2004 was given as $267,884 billion, whereas the real GDP for the first quarter of 2005 was given as $278,045 billion. Nominal GDP for the first quarter of 2004 was $301,137 billion, and the nominal GDP for the first quarter of 2005 was $319,833.

Year	Nominal GDP	Real GDP
2004	$301,137	$267,884
2005	$319,833	$278,045

a) What is the value of the change in production? $= \Delta Real\ GDP$.
To find the value of the change in production, the change in real GDP is needed.
$278,045 - 267,884 = 10,161$ billion
The value of the change in production is $10,161 billion.

b) State the growth rate of real GDP.
The growth rate of real GDP $= \dfrac{[278,045 - 267,884]}{267,884} * 100$
$= 3.79\%$

c) What is the value of the GDP deflator for the first quarter of 2004?
(i) GDP deflator for the first quarter of 2004 $= \dfrac{301,137}{267,884} * 100$ $\frac{P \times Q}{Q}$
$= 112.4$

c) What is the value of the GDP deflator for the first quarter of 2005?
(ii) GDP deflator for the first quarter of 2005 $= \dfrac{319,833}{278,045} * 100$
$= 115.03$

d) State the inflation rate between the first quarter of 2005 and the first quarter of 2004 using the GDP deflator.
The inflation rate $= \dfrac{[P_2 - P_1]}{P_1} * 100$
$= \dfrac{[115.03 - 112.4]}{112.4} * 100$
$= 2.34\%$

True/False:

1. The change in Capital Stock is positive if Gross Investment is increasing.
Gross Investment = Net Investment + Depreciation
The change in Capital Stock is positive, if Net Investment is increasing.
False

2. Gross domestic income at factor cost includes wages and salaries plus interest plus business profits plus depreciation plus indirect taxes minus subsidies.
   The preceding statement describes gross domestic income at market prices. Indirect taxes need to be removed and subsidies added when dealing with factor prices.
   False

Problems:

1. You are given the following information about the economy of Moose Bottom (all figures are in millions of dollars):

Depreciation	= $30	Consumption	= $200
Savings	= $275	Exports	= $150
Net investment	= $70	Wages and salaries	= $300
Transfer payments	= $90	Imports	= $50
Subsidies	= $10	Interest	= $50
Taxes	= $25		
Government expenditures	= $100		

Gross investment = net investment + Depreciation.

   a) What is the value of real GDP in Moose Bottom?
   $$Y = C + I + G + X - IM$$
   $$= 200 + 100 + 100 + 150 - 50$$
   $$= 500$$
   The value of real GDP in Moose Bottom is $500 million.

   NDI
   b) State the value of net domestic income at factor costs in the economy of Moose Bottom.
   GDP=NDI + Tax - subsidies + Depreciation
   At market prices GDP = GDI
   NDI = GDI − depreciation − taxes + subsidies
   NDI = 500 − 30 − 25 + 10
   NDI = 455
   Net domestic income at factor costs in the economy of Moose Bottom is $455 million.

   c) What is the value of national asset formation?
   nation asset formation
   Nation asset formation = I + (X − IM)
   = Gross investment + (Export - Import)
   = 100 + (150 − 50)
   = 200

   d) What is the value of national savings?
   National savings = S + (T − G)
   National Saving = Saving + (Taxes - Government)
   = 275 + (25 − 100)
   = 200

39

e) What relationship have you discovered between part (b), the value of national asset formation, and part (c), the value of national savings?
National asset formation = National savings = 200

2. Following is the data for the economy of Bella Venezia, where there are three final goods and services produced: Pizza, Vino (Wine), and Gondola Rides.

	Current Year Output	Current Period		Base Period	
		Price	Exp.	Price	Exp.
Pizza (each)	10,000	$10	$100,000	$ 8	$ 80,000
Vino (Wine) (bottles)	6,000	$30	$180,000	$25	$150,000
Gondola Rides (each)	5,000	$50	$250,000	$40	$200,000
Total Expenditure			$530,000		$430,000

a) Calculate the total expenditures for this economy at both base and current year prices.

b) What is the value of nominal GDP in the current period?
$530,000

c) What is the value of real GDP in the current period?
$430,000

d) What is the GDP deflator in the current period?
$\frac{\text{Nominal GDP}}{\text{Real GDP}} * 100 = \frac{530,000}{430,000} * 100 = 123.26$

3. You are given the following information about the economy of Mystery Heights (all figures are in billions of dollars):

Consumption = $4190   Depreciation = $175
Interest = $300   Exports = $485
Net investment = $1125   Wages and salaries = $5,500
Imports = $495   Subsidies = $35 $5500 + 625 + 300$
Government expenditures = $1250   Business profits = $625
Indirect taxes = $165

a) Find the value of real gross domestic product at market prices.

$$Y = C + I + G + X - IM$$
$$\text{Real GDP} = 4190 + (1125 + 175) + 1250 + 485 - 495 \quad eg). \text{ Expenditure approach}$$
$$= 6730$$

The value of real GDP at market prices is $6730 billion.

b) Find the value of gross domestic income at market prices.   income approach

$$\text{GDI} = \text{wages and salaries} + \text{interest} + \text{business profits} + \text{depreciation}$$
$$+ \text{indirect taxes} - \text{subsidies}$$
$$\text{GDI} = 5500 + 300 + 625 + 175 + 165 - 35$$
$$= 6730$$

The value of real gross domestic income at market prices is $6730 billion.

c) What is the value of net domestic income at factor cost?

$$\text{NDI} = \text{wages and salaries} + \text{interest} + \text{business profits} \quad \text{note Us}.$$
$$\text{NDI} = 5500 + 300 + 625$$
$$= 6425$$

or,

$$\text{NDI} = \text{GDI} - \text{depreciation} - \text{indirect taxes} + \text{subsidies}$$
$$\text{NDI} = 6730 - 175 - 165 + 35$$
$$= 6425$$

The value of net domestic income at factor cost is $6425 billion.

1. $Y_D = Y$ (real income) $- T_{(tax)}$

2. $Y_D = C + S_{(saving)}$

3. Avg. Propensity to consume $= \frac{C}{Y_D} = APC$

Marginal propensity to consume $= \frac{\Delta C}{\Delta Y_D} = MPC$

4. Avg. Propensity to save $= \frac{S}{Y_D} = APS$

Marginal propensity to save $= \frac{\Delta S}{\Delta Y_D} = MPS$

5. $MPC + MPS = 1$; $APC + APS = 1$

Assignment #3: Desired Aggregate Expenditure

Multiple Choice:

1. In general, the consumption function shows that as disposable income increases, consumption

6. The simple multiplier $= \frac{1}{1-MPC}$ [e]

   a) falls and savings rise.
   b) and savings are both constant.
   c) is constant and savings fall.
   d) is constant and savings rise.
   e) and savings will both rise.

7. The consumption Function $\Rightarrow$ $C = a + MPC \cdot Y_D$

   Autonomous.

   $Y_D = C + S$

   disposable income $\uparrow = C\uparrow + S\uparrow$

2. If a typical household's disposable income rose from $45,000 to $50,000 and their desired consumption expenditures also rose from $27,000 to $29,800, we can conclude that

   [e]

   a) marginal propensity to save is 0.56.
   b) average propensity to save is 0.56.
   c) marginal propensity to consume is $2,800.
   d) average propensity to consume is 0.56.
   e) marginal propensity to consume is 0.56.

   $MPC = \frac{\Delta C}{\Delta Y_D}$

   $= \frac{29800-27000}{50000-45000} = \frac{2800}{5000} = 0.56$

2. Savings is measured as disposable income minus

   [d]

   a) net taxes.
   b) net taxes plus subsidies.
   c) average savings.
   d) consumption expenditure.
   e) transfer payments.

3. Disposable income is

   [b]

   a) equal to consumption minus savings.
   b) equal to consumption expenditures plus savings.
   c) equal to real gross domestic product minus consumption.
   d) equal to real gross domestic product plus savings.
   e) equal to real gross domestic product minus transfer payments.

   $C > Y_D$ mean dis saving (borrow)

   $C < Y_D$ mean saving

   $C = Y_D$

4. The marginal propensity to consume is calculated as $MPC = \frac{\Delta C}{\Delta Y_D}$ [c]

   a) total consumption divided by the change in disposable income.
   b) total consumption divided by the change in real gross domestic product.
   c) the change in total consumption divided by the change in total disposable income.
   d) the change in marginal consumption divided by the change in total disposable income.
   e) total consumption divided by total disposable income.

5. If the consumption function lies above the 45 45-degree reference line, households
   a) are dissaving. [a]
   b) are consuming all their disposable income.
   c) are saving more than they are consuming.
   d) are saving all their disposable income.
   e) are consuming less than they are saving.

6. The multiplier process describes changes that occur in [c]
   a) autonomous expenditure brought about by a change in income.
   b) induced expenditure brought about by a change in disposable income.
   c) the equilibrium level of income caused by changes in autonomous expenditure.
   d) investment expenditure brought about by a change in real gross domestic product.
   e) autonomous expenditure brought about by changes in the price level.

$$K = \frac{1}{1-z} = \frac{\Delta A}{\Delta A} \cdot \frac{\Delta Y}{\Delta A} \quad \therefore \Delta Y = \Delta A \cdot k$$

↳ mp to spend

True/False:

1. Disposable income is the income that households have left after paying for basic expenses such as food and housing.
   Real GDP minus net taxes equals disposable income.

$$Y - T = Yd$$

   This disposable income is either consumed or saved.

$$Yd = C + S$$

   False

2. Real gross domestic product is equal to consumption expenditures plus savings.

   Real GDP equals consumption expenditures plus savings plus net taxes.

$$Y = C + S + T$$

   False

$$Y_D = Y - T$$
$$Y_D = C + S$$
$$\Rightarrow Y = C + S + T$$

Problems:

1. Welcome to the economy of Spend-it-up Village. Given in the following schedule is disposable income and consumption for this economy.

dissaving

Yd	C	S
0	100	−100
500	550	−50
1000	1000	0
1500	1450	50
2000	1900	100
2500	2350	150
3000	2800	200

(handwritten annotations: Yd column: 500, 500, 500, ΔYd=500; C column: 450, 450, 450, 450, ΔC=450; S column: 50, 50, 50, 50, ΔS=50)

a) From this information, fill in the column for savings.

b) State the value of the marginal propensity to consume out of disposable income.

$$MPC_{Yd} = \frac{\Delta C}{\Delta Yd} = \frac{450}{500} = 0.9$$

c) What is the value of the autonomous component of consumption?
   When Yd = 0 then a = 100

$$C = a + MPC \cdot YD$$

d) Write the consumption function.

autonomous / marginal propensity consumption.

$$C = a + bYd$$
$$C = 100 + 0.9Yd$$

e) State the value of the marginal propensity to save out of disposable income.

$$MPS_{Yd} = \frac{\Delta S}{\Delta Yd} = \frac{50}{500} = 0.1$$

OR "1 − marginal propensity to consume"

f) What is the value of the autonomous component of savings?
   When Yd = 0 then a = −100

autonomous component of saving = Negative to autonomous component of consumption.

g) Write the savings function.

$$S = -a + (1 - b)Yd$$
$$S = -100 + 0.1Yd$$

$$S = -a + MPS \cdot Y_D$$
$$= -a + (1 - MPC) \cdot Y_D$$

45

$Yd = c + s$

$MPC_{Yd} + MPS_{Yd} = 1$

h) What are the similarities between these two functions?

$\underline{Yd = C + S}$ and $\underline{MPC_{Yd} + MPS_{Yd} = 1}$

$Yd = (a + bYd) + [-a + (1 - b)Yd]$

$Yd = (100 + 0.9Yd) + (-100 + 0.1Yd)$

$Yd = 1Yd$

Also, $Yd - C = S$

$Yd - (a + bYd) = [-a + (1 - b)Yd]$

2. In the economy of Badgerville, the simplified aggregate expenditure function
($AE = C + I$) in millions is given as: $AE = 250 + 0.6Y$

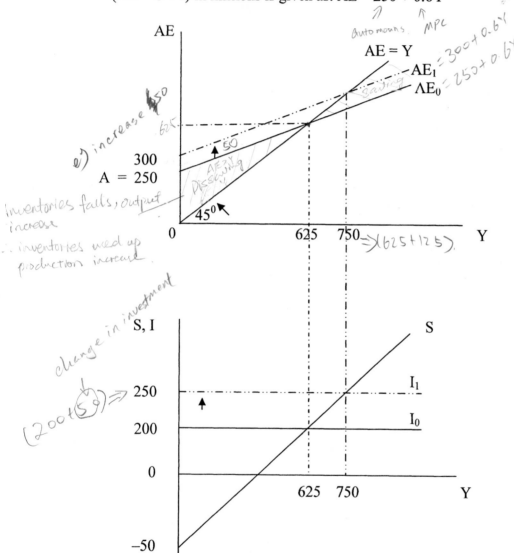

autonomous. MPC

$AE_1 = 300 + 0.6Y$

$AE_0 = 250 + 0.6Y$

Saving

e') increase

50

625

$AE = Y$

$AE > Y$
Dissaving

50

300

A = 250

$45°$

Inventories falls, output increase

∴ inventories used up
production increase.

0   625   750→(625+125)   Y

change in investment

(200(59))⇒

S, I   S

250   I_1

200   I_0

0

625   750

Y

−50

a) Find the equilibrium level of real GDP. $AE = Y$

Total spending = Total income.

In equilibrium $AE = Y$

$Y = 250 + 0.6Y$

$(1 - 0.6)Y = 250$

$0.4\,Y = 250$

$Y = 250 / 0.4$

$Y = 625$

Real GDP in equilibrium is $625 million.

b) Show this level of real gross domestic product on both of the preceding graphs.

c) State the value of the simple multiplier. *Simple multiplier $= \dfrac{K}{1 - MPC}$*

[$z = 0.6$]

$K = \dfrac{1}{1 - \text{(z)}} = \dfrac{1}{1 - 0.6} = \dfrac{1}{0.4} = 2.5$

Simple multiple   *slope of AE*

The simple fixed-price multiplier is 2.5.

d) If investment increases by 50, what is the change in real GDP that will result?

$K = \dfrac{\Delta Y}{\Delta I}$

$\Delta I = +50$ $K = 2.5$ *∴ the Δln real GDP = ΔInvestment + the simple multiplier.*

$\Delta I \times K = \Delta Y$

$+50 \times 2.5 = +125$ *= 50 x 2·5*

$\Delta Y = +125$ *= 125*

The change in real GDP is an increase of $125 million.

e) Show the change in investment and the change in aggregate expenditures on the preceding diagrams.

f) What is the value of the marginal propensity to save?

$MPC + MPS = 1$

$1 - MPC = MPS$

$1 - 0.6 = 0.4$

The marginal propensity to save out of real GDP is 0.4.

chapter 22:

1. Taxes: $T = ty$; $t = $ tax rate

2. Imports, $Im = mY$ $m = $ marginal Propensity to import.

$$Y_D = Y - T$$
$$\Rightarrow Y_D = Y - tY$$
$$\Rightarrow Y_D = Y(1-t)$$

$\Rightarrow$ multiplier $= \dfrac{1}{1 - \text{slope of}} $ HE line.

3. Multiplier $= \dfrac{1}{1 - [mpc(1-t) - m]}$

4. Tax Multiplier $= \dfrac{-mpc}{1 - [mpc(1-t) - m]}$

5. Δ In the autonomous Expenditures $\times$ multiplier $= \Delta$ In Real GDP

we know that: $AE = C + I + G + x - IM$

$$\underset{(m \cdot Y)}{\downarrow}$$

$$\Rightarrow AE = a + MPC \cdot Y(1-t) + I + G + x - mY$$

$$\Rightarrow AE = a + I + G + x + MPC \cdot Y(1-t) - mY$$

$$AE = (a + I + G + x) + Y[MPC(1-t) - m]$$

$$\Rightarrow AE = \text{Autonomous Expenditures} + Y[MPC(1-t) - m]$$
$$\underset{\hookrightarrow \text{the slope of } AE \text{ function.}}{}$$

Now: $C = a + MPC \cdot Y_D$

$$\underset{\text{autonomous consumption}}{\downarrow}$$

$$\rightarrow C = a + MPC \cdot Y(1-t)$$

EQ. For straight line: $Y = mx + b$
$$\downarrow$$
$$AE = [mpc(1-t) - m] \cdot Y + Aut.$$

Assignment #4: Introducing Government and Trade

Multiple Choice:

1. The presence of induced taxes means   [e]
   a) fiscal policy multipliers are made larger.
   b) discretionary fiscal policy is weakened.
   c) there is always a deficit.
   d) there are no transfer payments.
   e) fluctuations in aggregate expenditure are reduced.

2. A rise in the domestic price level will   [d]
   a) increase the level of desired aggregate expenditures.
   b) decrease desired aggregate expenditures only if household incomes change.
   c) cause net exports to rise.
   d) decrease desired aggregate expenditures because the real value of wealth would change.
   e) have no effect on the level of desired aggregate expenditures.

3. Assuming a constant price level, an increase in autonomous expenditures will cause the AE curve to shift   [d]
   a) upward and the aggregate demand curve shifts leftward.
   b) downward and a movement rightward along the aggregate demand curve.
   c) downward and the aggregate demand curve shifts leftward.
   d) upward and the aggregate demand curve shifts rightward.
   e) downward and the aggregate demand curve shifts rightward.

4. The automatic fiscal stabilizers that affect aggregate expenditures are [b]
   a) autonomous taxation.
   b) progressive income taxes and employment insurance payments.
   c) government purchases of goods and services.
   d) interest rates and exchange rates.
   e) the marginal propensity to consume.

5. The autonomous tax multiplier   [b]
   a) has the same value as the government expenditures multiplier during recessions and inflations.
   b) is smaller than the government expenditures multiplier.
   c) is larger than the government expenditures multiplier.
   d) is larger than the government expenditures multiplier at potential GDP.
   e) and the government expenditures multiplier are always equal.

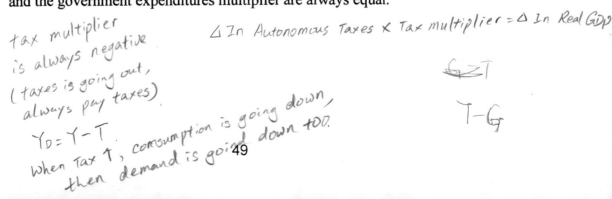

49

True/False:

1. Fiscal policy is more effective if the slope of the AE line is low.
$z = MPCy - MPM$ If $MPCy \downarrow$ or $MPM \uparrow$ then, $z \downarrow$

$K = \dfrac{1}{1-z}$ If $z \downarrow$ then, $[1-z] \uparrow$  $\left[\dfrac{1}{1-z}\right] \downarrow$ ∴ $K \downarrow$

There is a direct relationship between the marginal propensity to spend and the multiplier; therefore, as marginal propensity to spend becomes flatter, the multiplier also decreases.

ΔG or ΔT multiplied by a smaller multiplier will yield a smaller result.
Fiscal policy would then be less effective.

False   *if slope of AE line is low ⇒ multiplier is low.*

and Δ ln Autonomous expenditures × multiplier = Δ ln Real Y is low too

2. The multiplier is larger when the aggregate supply curve is upward sloping.
When the aggregate supply curve is horizontal, the price level is constant; however, with an upward sloping supply curve, the price level increases as we move up along aggregate supply.

With any given change in autonomous expenditures, say government expenditures, the change in real GDP will be less when prices increase.

The fixed-price multiplier is larger than the variable-priced multiplier for any given change in autonomous expenditure.

$K = \dfrac{Y_1 - Y_0}{\Delta G} > K = \dfrac{Y_2 - Y_0}{\Delta G}$

Aggregate Supply (AS) curve can Be:
upward sloping; Horizontal ⇒ (Fixed Price level)
↑ Δ ln Autonomous Expenditure × Multiplier = Δ ln Real Y

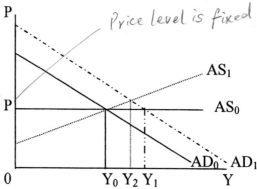

Price level is fixed

False

Problems:

1. The economy of Aviator Lake, given in billions of dollars per year, is as follows:
Autonomous consumption = 80
Marginal propensity to consume = 0.9
Investment = 200
Government expenditure = 200
Exports = 250
Imports = $0.21Y$
Net taxes = $0.1Y$

$= AE$

a) State the value of the aggregate expenditure function.

Step 1: *income* Solve for Yd

Yd = Y – T *+ tax*

Yd = 1Y – 0.1Y

Yd = 0.9Y

Step 2: Substitute Yd = 0.9Y into the consumption function

C = 80 + 0.9Yd

C = 80 + 0.9 (0.9Y)

C = 80 + 0.81Y

Step 3: Substitute the transformed consumption function into the aggregate expenditure function and solve.

AE = C + I + G + X – IM

AE = 80 + 0.81Y + 200 + 200 + 250 – 0.21Y

AE = 730 + 0.6Y

↳ $mpc(1-t)-m$.

b) Find the value of equilibrium expenditure.

In equilibrium AE = Y

$\qquad$ Y = 730 + 0.6Y $\qquad$ * Remember the numerical co efficient of Y is 1.

[1 – 0.6] Y = 730

$\qquad$ 0.4Y = 730

$\qquad$ Y = 730/0.4

$\qquad$ Y_E = 1825

Real GDP in equilibrium is $1825 billion.

$\left(multiplier = \dfrac{1}{1-[mpc\,(1-t)-m]} = \dfrac{1}{1-0.6} = 2.5 \right)$

c) If investment expenditures are increased to 300, what is the subsequent change in real GDP?

To 300 ⟹ ΔI = + 100

The multiplier is $K = \dfrac{1}{1-z} = \dfrac{1}{1-0.6} = \dfrac{1}{0.4} = 2.5 = $ Δ In Real Y.

Δ In Auto. Exp × Multiplier

ΔI = 300 – 200 = 100

$\qquad$ ΔI * K = ΔY

+ 100 * 2.5 = + 250

The change in real GDP is an increase of $250 billion.

d) Given the level of equilibrium real GDP found in part (b) and with the value of potential real GDP equal to 1600 [Y* = 1600], what change in exports might be needed to close this output gap?

Step 1:

The output gap is ΔY = Y* – Y_E = 1600 – 1825 = –225 $\left(Output\ gap = Potential\ GDP - Real\ GDP \right)$

This is an inflationary gap of $225 billion.

Note: The output gap is ΔY = Y – Y_E differs from the text book; however, in aggregate expenditure problems, this is the superior method.

Step 2:

The multiplier is K = 2.5 as found in part (c).

Step 3:
$$\Delta X = \frac{\Delta Y}{K} = \frac{-225}{2.5} = -90$$

The change in exports is a decrease of $90 billion.
*Note: There is no change in the price level.

e) On the aggregate demand and aggregate supply diagram and also on the aggregate expenditure diagram, draw the original or beginning position of the price level, real GDP, and state the value of autonomous expenditures.

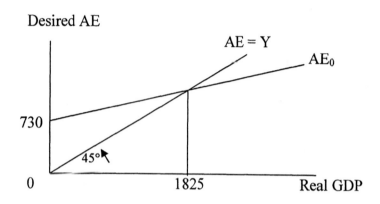

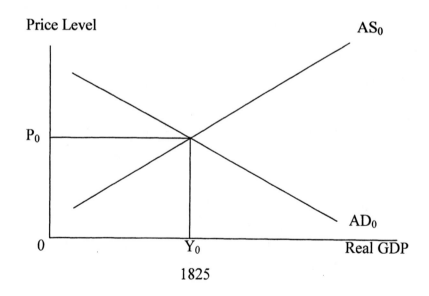

f) On the aggregate demand and aggregate supply diagram and also on the aggregate expenditure diagram, show the changes that result from a change in exports.

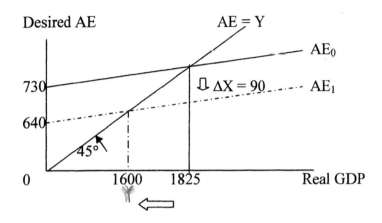

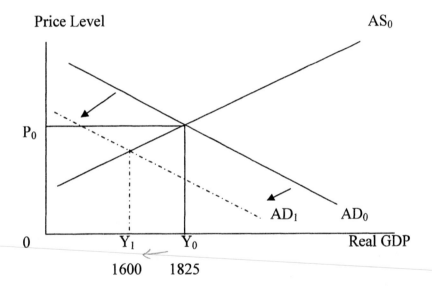

g) Show the decrease in the price level on the aggregate expenditure graph.

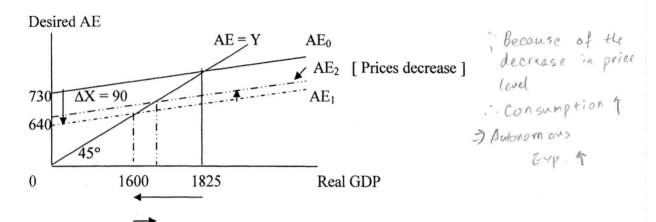

Because of the decrease in price level

∴ Consumption ↑

⇒ Autonomous Exp. ↑

h) Δ In Auto. Taxes × Tax Multiplier = Δ In Real GDP

If government expenditures remained at \$200 and autonomous taxes were increased by \$100, what change would result in real GDP?

$\Delta T = +100$ $K_T = \dfrac{-b}{1-z} = \dfrac{-0.9}{1-0.6} = \dfrac{-0.9}{0.4} = -2.25$

$\Delta T * K_T = \Delta Y$

$+100 * -2.25 = -225$

or,

$$K_T = \dfrac{-MPC_{YD}}{1-z}$$

Tax multiplier

Real GDP would decrease by \$225 billion.

i) The tax multiplier is given by $K_T = \dfrac{-b}{1-z}$

Why is –b used in the numerator?
Taxes work through disposable income and disposable income is either consumed or saved. That portion of disposable income that is consumed is done so according to one's marginal propensity to consume out of disposable income, MPC_{Yd} or b. There is an inverse relationship between disposable income and taxation. The more one is taxed, the less disposable income is available; consequently, the negative sign is placed before the marginal propensity to consume.

j) State the formula for the transfer payments multiplier.

$$K_{TR} = \dfrac{b}{1-z} \quad \text{or,} \quad \dfrac{MPC_{YD}}{1-z}.$$

54

2. The following schedule relates to the economy of Carnival Bay (in billions of dollars).

real GDP   *autonomous*

Y	C	I	G	X	IM	AE
0	50	50	60	60	0	220
100	110	50	60	60	15	265
200	170	50	60	60	30	310
300	230	50	60	60	45	355
400	290	50	60	60	60	400
500	350	50	60	60	75	445
600	410	50	60	60	90	490

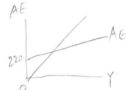

a) Fill in the preceding chart.

b) State the value of autonomous expenditure.
   When Y = 0, A = 220

c) State the value of the marginal propensity to consume out of real GDP.
   $MPC_Y = \Delta C / \Delta Y = 60/100 = 0.6$

d) When real GDP is equal to 200, what is the value of aggregate expenditures?
   When Y = 200, AE = 310

e) Discuss the situation that exists at this level with respect to inventories and the ensuing production decisions.
   Y = 200, AE = 310
   This economy is selling more than it is producing.
   AE > Y
   Y – AE = 200 – 310 = –110
   Inventories are depleting. This economy should increase production.

   AE (selling)   Y (producing)
   ∴ selling is more than producing → the economy should increase production.

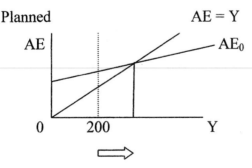

f) When real GDP is equal to 500, what is the value of aggregate expenditure?
   When Y = 500, AE = 445

55

g) Discuss the situation that exists at this new level with respect to inventories and the ensuing production decisions.

Y = 500, AE = 445

This economy is producing more than it is selling.

AE < Y

Y − AE = 500 − 445 = +55

Inventories are accumulating. This economy should <u>decrease production</u>.

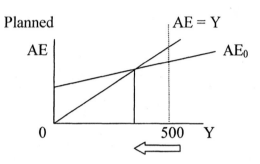

h) State the value of the marginal propensity to import.

MPM = $\Delta m/\Delta Y$ = 15/100 = 0.15

i) Find the slope of the aggregate expenditure [AE] equation, which is the marginal propensity to spend [z].

$$slope = \frac{rise}{run} = \frac{\Delta \ln AE}{\Delta \ln Y}$$

__Method # 1__

z = $\Delta AE / \Delta Y$

z = 45/100

z = 0.45

0 < z < 1

or, __Method # 2__

MPC_Y = 0.6 (consumer)   MPM = 0.15 (import)

z = MPC_Y − MPM

z = 0.6 − 0.15

z = 0.45

or, __Method # 3__

z = b(1-t) − m

However, the information needed to complete this method is not provided in the given chart.

j) Find the value of the simple fixed-price multiplier [K].

K = $\dfrac{1}{1-z}$

K = $\dfrac{1}{1-0.45}$

K = $\dfrac{1}{0.55}$

K = 1.82

K > 1

Chapter 24:

1. output GAP = Potential GDP − Real GDP

i) inflationary Gap: When Real GDP > Potential GDP

ii) Recessionary GAP: when Real GDP < Potential GDP

2. Positive Demand SHOCK:

⟹ Inflationary GAP

⟹ Price level ↑

⟹ Unemployment < Natural Rate of employment

⟹ Wage Rate increase

⟹ Production Ra costs ↑

⟹ AS ↓ (AS Curve shifts left)

⟹ Real GDP Back to Y* (potential)

⟹ Price level future ↑ to P_2

Assignment #5: Aggregate Demand, Aggregate Supply, and the Price Level

Multiple Choice:

1. Which of the following does **not** affect aggregate demand?   [d]
   a) changes in expected future income
   b) changes in fiscal policy
   c) changes in monetary policy
   d) changes in technological change   *technology affect AS*
   e) changes in the exchange rate

2. Ceteris paribus, all else remaining the same, potential GDP increases with a(n) [b]
   a) decrease in the labour force.
   b) advance in technology.
   c) decrease in capital stock.
   d) fall in wages.
   e) drop in the price level.

   self adjustment. machine
   inflation gap
   - tight labour market
   - wage ↑

3. An output gap occurs in the economy when
   a) nominal GDP is greater than the real GDP.
   b) demand for labour is high.
   c) actual GDP and potential GDP differ.
   d) potential national income is greater than equilibrium national income.
   e) actual GDP equals potential GDP.

   [c]

   G↑ ⇒ AD ↑.
   AD ⇒ Inflation GAP.

True/False: *G↑*

1. If government expenditures are increased in an economy that is presently in long-run
   equilibrium, the resulting change in real gross domestic product will be permanent. *will change back*
   If government purchases are increased when an economy is at potential GDP,
   aggregate demand will increase and real GDP will increase. Real GDP is now greater
   than potential GDP. An inflationary gap has developed. The economy does not
   remain at this increased level of real GDP because the tight labour market would
   cause wages to rise, unit production costs to rise, and the aggregate supply curve to
   shift leftward, increasing prices and moving real GDP back to potential GDP.
   The change in real GDP is temporary.
   False

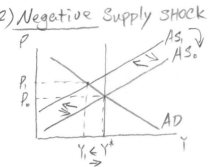

2) Negative Supply SHOCK

⇒ Production Costs ↓
⇒ AS ↑; Shifts Right
⇒ Price level ↓ To P₀ ;
* Real Y back to Y†*

⇒ Recessionary GAP
⇒ Unemployment Rate > Natural rate level of U.
⇒ wages Rate ↓

57

AS WV.
V. AS, CV.
P
P
AO
Real GDP

P
P
AS
ADi
AD.
Real GDP

Expantioniary Fiscal Policy
(G↑, ↓T×)

2. Fiscal policy provides a speedier recovery from a recession than does the self-adjustment mechanism.

Expansionary fiscal policy may be necessary to eliminate a recessionary gap. Government expenditures increase or taxes decrease to increase aggregate demand and real GDP.

The self-adjustment mechanism requires wages to decrease to increase the aggregate supply curve and real GDP; however, wages are sticky downward, and wages could take a considerable length of time to decline.

Fiscal policy is a speedier solution.

True

P_1
P_0
As
AD,
AD,

AD shift to right because of fiscal policy Expendition.

Problems:

Price Level

P_0
Y^*

P_0
P_1
AS_0
AS_1
A_0

P↓ AD↑

AS_0

AD_0

0   Y^* Real GDP
           ↑ potential GDP.

1. The economy of Snowtown is initially in long-run equilibrium. Please analyze the following actions on the price level and real GDP as the economy moves to a new equilibrium position. Explain both graphically and verbally.
(Hint: Draw a new diagram for each example.)

a) The nominal wage rate increases in Snowtown.   [W ↑]

Price Level

=> Production costs ↑
=> Supply curve AS shift to left   } => Recessionary GAP.
=> Price level up to P₁
=> Real GDP ↓ to Y₁

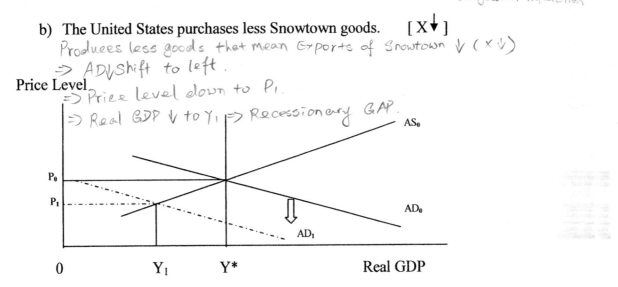

AS₁
AS₀

⇧ P₁
P₀

AD₀

0

real GDP Y₁   Y* potential Gdp   Real GDP

At Y_1, there is a recessionary gap. Real GDP is less than potential GDP. Unemployment is above the natural rate of unemployment. Price level has increased. Stagflation now exists.

stagflation inflation

b) The United States purchases less Snowtown goods.   [X ↓]

Produces less goods that mean Exports of Snowtown ↓ (X ↓)
=> AD↓ shift to left.

Price Level
=> Price level down to P₁.
=> Real GDP ↓ to Y₁ => Recessionary GAP.

AS₀

P₀

P₁
                                    AD₀
                    ⇩
              AD₁

0   Y₁   Y*   Real GDP

At Y_1, there is a recessionary gap. Exports have decreased. Real GDP is less than potential GDP. Unemployment is above the natural rate of unemployment. Price level has decreased.

59

c) Government expenditures in Snowtown increase.   [G ↑]

Price Level

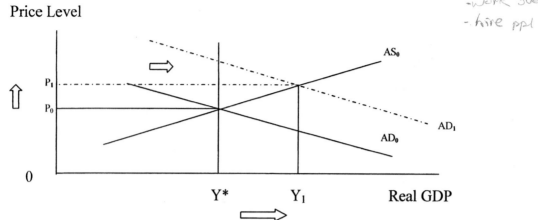

At Y_1, there is an inflationary gap. Real GDP is greater than potential GDP. Unemployment is below the natural rate of unemployment. Price level has increased.

AS.
output per person per hour

d) Snowtown productivity increases.   *Productivity ↑ : AS ↑*
=> Price level ↓ to P_1
=> Real Y ↑ to Y_1
=> Inflationary GAP

Price Level

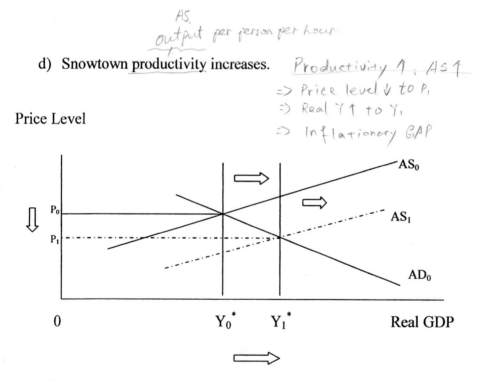

At Y_1^*, the economy is at a higher level of potential GDP. The short-run supply curve has shifted rightward. The long-run supply curve has also shifted rightward. AD_0 equals AS_1 equals Y_1^*. Real GDP is equal to the new level of potential GDP. Unemployment has fallen. Unemployment is at a new higher natural rate of unemployment. More people are employed at this new higher natural rate of unemployment. Price level has decreased.

Price Level

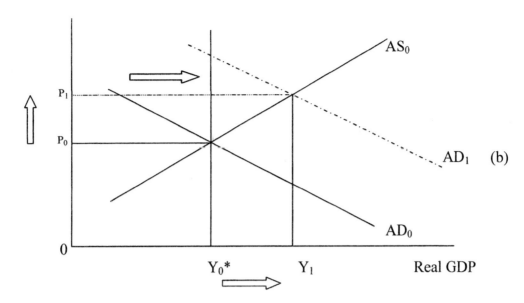

$$AD = C + I + S + X - CI$$

2. Preceding is the economy of Springtime.
   a) Describe the state of the economy of Springtime as depicted in the preceding
      graph.   *inflation gap...*
      Long-run equilibrium (at full employment). $Y = Y^*$

   b) If investment increased in this economy, label the new price level P_1 and the new
      Real GDP Y_1. Is the economy stable at this new equilibrium level? Explain.   *Investment Expendi*
      At the new level, an inflationary gap exists. This is not a stable situation. The   *increase*
      economy is experiencing a boom. Unemployment is below the natural rate of   *AD↑ ⇒ shift right*
      unemployment. People are working two jobs or working overtime.   *Price level ↑*
                                                                        Real GDP ↑ ⇒ to Y_1
                                                                        ⇒ Inflationary GAP
   c) After the change in investment, if the economy were left to its own devices   *Unemployment level*
      without interference from the government or the Central Bank of Springtime, at   *is less than natural*
      the new price, P_1, and new Real GDP, Y_1, what would you expect to happen?   *Rate of unemployment.*
      Explain.
      The tight labour market causes labour to demand higher nominal wages.   *self adjustment machi*
      Production costs increase.
      Short-run aggregate supply curve decreases; it shifts leftward.
      Real GDP decreases back to potential GDP, the full-employment level.
      Price level increases further.

      Wages level ↑.
      production cost ↑.
      AS ↓ ⇒ shift left until potential.
      ⇒ price level in furture to P_2
      ⇒ Real Y Back to to Y^* (Potential Y)

61

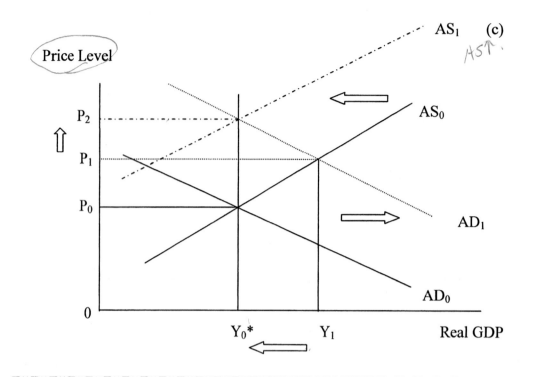

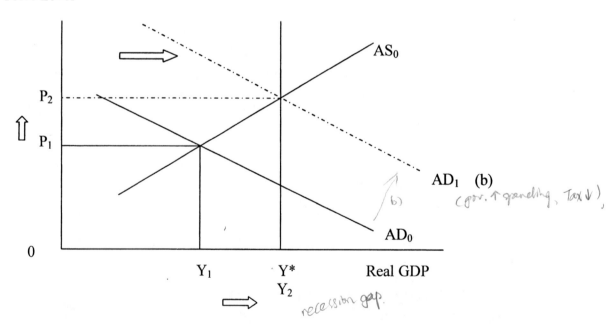

3. Preceding is the economy of Sorokaville.

R.g,   Expansionary fiscal policy.
(gov ↑ spending, Tax ↓)
Contratonary

a) Describe the state of the economy of Sorokaville as depicted in the graph above.
Recessionary Gap ∴ $Y < Y^*$ ∴ Recessionary GAP.

b) If government expenditures increased (to close the output gap) in this economy, label the new price level P_2 and the new Real GDP Y_2. Is the economy stable at this new equilibrium level? Explain.

∴ $G\uparrow$
- $AD\uparrow$
shift right
⟶ Price ↑ to P_2
⟶ Real GDP↑
to $Y_2=Y^*$
(Back to Y^*)
⟹ State
stable

If government purchases increased sufficiently to bring the economy back to potential GDP, this would be a stable economy. This action by the government is called expansionary fiscal policy.

c) If the economy was still at Y_1 and did not experience interference from the government or the Central Bank of Sorokaville, what would you expect to happen? Explain.

self adjustment machines

Real GDP is below potential GDP.
Unemployment is above the natural rate.
The economy is sluggish.
Expect nominal wages to decrease slowly.
Short-run aggregate supply increases, shifts rightward.
Real GDP increases back to potential GDP.
Price level decreases.

∨ Recessionary GAP.

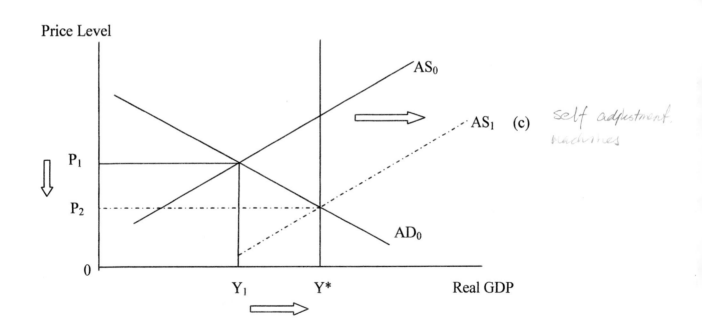

Price Level

P_1

P_2

AS_0

AS_1 (c) self adjustment machines

AD_0

0

Y_1 Y^* Real GDP

Chapter 23:-

1. The AD curve :- For a given Price level, any change in autonomous Expenditures will __SHIFT__ the AD curve.

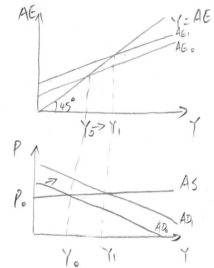

2. The AS curve :- any given in input Prices or Productivity will __SHIFt__ the AS curve.

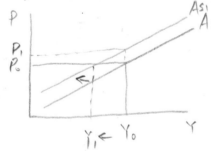

If - Input prices ↑ or Productivity ↓
⇒ AS will shift Left.

3. KEYNESIAN AS curve :-

(Price doesn't effect the AE, only AD effect the Real GDP).

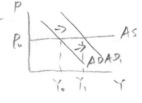

1. Deposit Multiplier, $DM = \frac{1}{V}$; $V =$ Target reserve ratio

2. Δ Deposits $= \frac{\Delta \text{Reserves}}{V}$

3. $\Delta MS = DM \times \Delta$ Deposits

4 With cash drain:
$$\Delta \text{Deposits} = \frac{\Delta \text{Reserves}}{C + V};$$
$C =$ Ratio of cash to deposits that people want to maintain.

<u>Assignment #6</u>: The Canadian Banking System

<u>Multiple Choice:</u>

5. kind of deposits:
i) $M1 =$ Currency + <u>Demand Deposits</u>

1. <u>Fiat money</u> is
   a) backed by gold.
   b) linked to the consumer price index.
   c) money that is decreed to be money by the government.

   No/little interest; chequable

   d) money used only to pay government employees.
   e) money given out by the car dealer, Fiat.

   ii) $M2 = M1 +$ Savings Deposits (higher Int, Non Chequable)

2. Which one of the following is the most widely accepted form of money?   [e]
   a) cheques, credit cards and debit cards
   b) cheques and debit cards
   c) fiat money and cheques
   d) fiat money and debit cards
   e) fiat money

   iii) $M2+ = M2 +$ Deposits Held at Institutions that are not Chartered Banks (e.g. asset management firms)

<u>True/False:</u>

Money Multiplier, $MM = \frac{1}{C+V}$
$V =$ The desired Reserve Ratio
$C =$ the cash drain.

1. An increase in the desired <u>reserve ratio</u> allows for greater money creation in the economy.

   Deposit multiple

   ← We know that $DM = \frac{1}{V}$
   ∴ Increase in target reserve
   Ratio ⟹ $V\uparrow$; $DM\downarrow$ Money creation is less

   reserve ratio $V \Uparrow \implies DM = \frac{1}{V} \Downarrow$

   The deposit multiplier is smaller, and therefore money creation is less.
   ∴ the statement is false

   <u>False</u>

<u>Problems:</u>

1. Pretty Polly Paul, a space cadet from Neptune and a cousin of Miss Tutu from Venus, immigrates to the country of New Canada. She brings along her life savings of $5,000. She deposits this money into the First National Bank of New Canada. The <u>reserve ratio [v] is 10%</u>, and there is <u>no cash drain.</u>

2.
   a) State the deposits multiplier [DM].
      $v = 10\% = 10/100 = 0.1$ $DM = \frac{1}{v} = \frac{1}{0.1} = 10$

22, 23, 24, 27

65

b) Fill in the following T-account showing the *initial effects* on the First National Bank of New Canada.

First National Bank of New Canada

Assets ₒwn		Liabilities oₙe
Reserves	+ $ 500	Demand Deposits + $5,000
Loans	+ $4,500	
Total	+ $5,000	Total + $5,000

c) Is this money creation or money destruction?
   Money creation

*Note:

$$v = 0.1$$
$$0.1* + \$5,000 = + \$ 500$$
$$\$5,000 - 500 = + \$4,500$$

d) In the following T-account, show the effect on the entire banking system in New Canada.

Flₓ

All Banks in New Canada

Assets		Liabilities
Reserves	+ $ 5,000	Deposits + $50,000 (10 x 5,000)
Loans	+ $45,000	(5000 x DM)
Total	+ $50,000	Total + $50,000

e) State the total change in reserves.
   Initial Reserves * DM = + $500 * 10 = + $5,000

f) What is the overall change in loans?
   Initial Loans * DM = + $4,500 * 10 = + $45,000

g) State the total change in deposits.
   Initial Deposit * DM = + $5,000 * 10 = + $50,000

66

h) What is the total change in the money supply? Has the money supply increased or decreased? Deposit multiple _change Deposit_

$$\Delta MS = \underline{DM} * \Delta \dot{D} \quad \text{or} \quad \left[\begin{array}{l} \Delta MS = DM * \Delta R \\ = 10 * +\$5,000 \\ = +\$50,000 \end{array} \right.$$

change money supply
$$= 10 * +\$5,000$$
$$= +\$50,000$$

*Note: ΔR is the *immediate* change in reserves, which is equal to the *immediate* change in deposits.

2. Prior to Ms. Paul entering the economy of New Canada, The First National Bank of New Canada had been a Monopoly bank, and its existing deposits were $3,000. It also had existing reserves of $300, and the bank was fully loaned out—no excess reserves.

Monopoly Bank of New Canada
*Note: Existing T-account prior to any additional deposits.

Assets		Liabilities	
Reserves	$ 300	Deposits	$3,000
Loans	$2,700		
Total	$3,000	Total	$3,000

What was the final change in the banking system in New Canada after Ms. Paul's deposit of $5,000? [10% target reserves] $\rightarrow$ $DM = \frac{1}{0.1} = 10$.

$\Delta Deposit / = DM \times Initial\ Deposit$
$= 10 \times 5000$
$= 50,000$

Monopoly Bank of New Canada
*Note: Represents the final changes in the banking system.

Assets		Liabilities	
Reserves	($5000 + 300) $ 5,300	Deposits	$53,000 (3000 + 50,000)
Loans	$47,700 (27,000 + 45,000)		
Total	$53,000	Total	$53,000

*Note: This is the middle step. The T-account is after the initial deposit and before the final deposit.

Monopoly Bank of New Canada

Assets		Liabilities	
Reserves	+ $ 500	Deposits	+ $5,000
Loans	+ $4,500		
Total	+ $5,000	Total	+ $5,000

$$\Delta MS = DM * \Delta D$$
$$= 10 * +\$5,000$$
$$= +\$50,000$$

3. Poor Polly Paul is homesick and decides to emigrate from New Canada and travel back to her home planet of Neptune. She finds New Canadians too liberal for her liking. Polly withdraws all her savings, $4,000, ready for her new adventure. The target reserve ratio is now 20%, and there is no cash drain.

   a) What is the value of the deposits multiplier?

   $$v = 0.2 \qquad DM = \frac{1}{v} = \frac{1}{0.2} = 5$$

   b) In the following T-account, show the *initial* result of this withdrawal from the First National Bank of New Canada.

First National Bank of New Canada

Assets		Liabilities	
Reserves	−$ 800 (told out)	Demand Deposits	−$4,000
Loans	−$3,200		The bank no longer exist.
Total	−$4,000	Total	−$4,000

   c) Is this money creation or money destruction?
   Money destruction

68

d) State the effect on the entire banking system in New Canada.

All Banks in New Canada

Assets		Liabilities	
Reserves	–$ 4,000 (5 x 800)	Deposits	–$20,000 (5x –4000)
Loans	–$16,000 (5 * 3200)		
Total	–$20,000	Total	–$20,000

e) What is the total change in the money supply? Has the money supply increased or decreased?

$$\Delta MS = DM * \Delta D \qquad \text{or,} \qquad \left[\begin{array}{l} \Delta MS = DM * \Delta R \\ \quad = 5 * -\$4{,}000 \\ \quad = -\$20{,}000 \end{array} \right.$$

$$= 5 * -\$4{,}000$$
$$= -\$20{,}000$$

4. Fill in the following chart showing the process of creating money when the desired reserve ratio is 10% and there is no cash drain.

Bank	Deposits	=	Reserves	+	Loans
A	$100		$ 10		$ 90
B	$ 90		$ 9		$ 81
C	$ 81		$ 8.10		$ 72.90
	:		:		:
Total	$ 1,000		$ 100		$ 900
	[10 * 100]		[10 * 10]		[10 * 90]

↳Original $100.   ↳Original $10.   ↳Original $90

*Note: The deposit multiplier is 10.

$$100 \times \left(\tfrac{1}{0.1}\right) =$$

5. The following shows the balance sheet of The Shady Bank with no excess reserves:

The Shady Bank

Assets		Liabilities	
Cash/Reserves	$\checkmark$ $ 100 + 10	Deposits	$1,000 +100
Loans	$1,100 + 90	Capital	$ 200
Total	$1,200	Total	$1,200

a) The bank now receives a new deposit of $100. Show the position of this bank after it has adjusted to the new deposit (assume no cash drain).

The Shady Bank

Desired reserve ratio = $\dfrac{Reserve}{Deposits} \times 100\%$.

Assets		Liabilities	
	$(100 + 100 \times 10\%)$		
Cash/Reserves	$ 110	Deposits	$1,100 ($(1000 + 100)$)
Loans	$1,190	Capital	$ 200
Total	$1,300	Total	$1,300

b) What is the final increase in bank deposits after the whole process is completed?

$$v = 0.1 \qquad DM = \frac{1}{v} = \frac{1}{0.1} = 10$$

$$\frac{+100 \times 10 = 1100}{1000}$$
$$\frac{1000}{100}$$

$$\Delta D = \text{Initial Deposit} * DM = +\$100 * 10 = +\$1,000 \qquad 100 \times 10 = 1000$$

c) What would the final increase in deposits be if there was a 10% cash drain?

$$mm = \frac{1}{c + v} = \frac{1}{0.1 + 0.1} = \frac{1}{0.2} = 5 \qquad \text{no deposit}$$

cash drain → c + v

$$\Delta D = \text{Initial Deposit} * mm = +\$100 * 5 = +\$500$$

$$\frac{1}{0.2} = 5$$

$$+ 5 \times 100 = 5\nu$$

*Note: DM is the deposits multiplier.
mm is the money multiplier.
v is the desired reserve ratio.
c is the cash drain.

70

Assignment #7: Bonds and the Monetary Transmission Mechanism

Multiple Choice:

1. If together all the banks in the banking system have $30 million in cash reserves and
   have a desired reserve ratio of 3%, the maximum amount of demand deposits the
   banking system can support is   [d]
   a) $9 million.
   b) $60 million.
   c) $90 million.
   d) $1 billion.
   e) $900 million.

   30,000,000 (handwritten above "$30 million")
   √ = 0.03 (handwritten)
   1000,000,000 (handwritten next to d)

2. Bond prices are   [e]
   a) directly related to interest rates.
   b) not affected by changes in money demand.
   c) directly related to the change in interest rates.
   d) not affected by changes in the interest rates.
   e) inversely related to interest rates.

3. If interest rates are expected to fall in the near future, a rational individual would be
   willing to   [a]
   a) buy bonds immediately.
   b) buy bonds only if their prices begin to fall.
   c) maintain only their current bond holdings.
   d) place their money into savings and not buy bonds.
   e) sell bonds immediately.

   interest rate ↓. Bond ↑ (handwritten)

True/False:

1. An increase in interest rates with a relatively flat investment demand curve is
   associated with a small increase in investment, aggregate demand and real GDP.
   Most often, a flat investment demand curve is associated with a fairly steep money
   demand curve.
   When interest rates increase, they move in tandem with the money supply, which
   decreases or shifts leftward. This given change in the interest rates is transmitted to
   the investment demand curve.

   The flatter the investment demand curve, the more sensitive that curve is to the
   changes in interest rates and the greater will be the changes in investment. As
   investment moves to the output market, a large change or decrease in investment will
   cause a large decrease in aggregate demand, aggregate expenditure, and real GDP.
   False

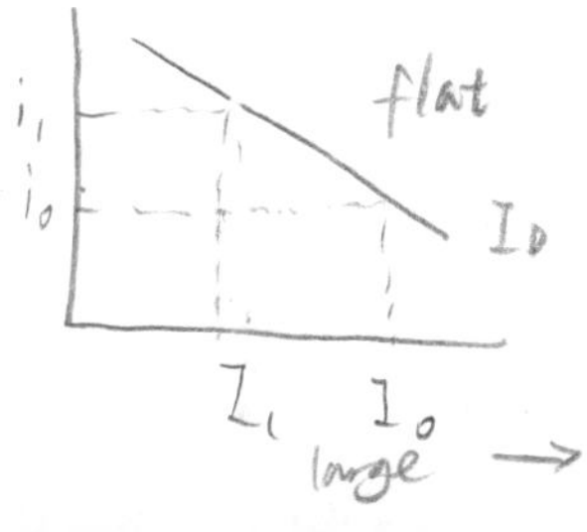

   (handwritten graph with "flat", "I_D", "I_1 I_0 large → ΔAD → ΔY")

   (handwritten notes on right:)
   if I_D is steep:
   ↳ smaller ΔI_D
   smaller ΔAD
   ΔY
   if I_D is flat
   ↳ larger ΔI_D
   ΔAD
   ΔY

71

ΔY
or $\Rightarrow$
ΔP M_D will change.

$\uparrow Y \rightarrow M_D \uparrow \rightarrow i \uparrow$

2. When real GDP increases, money demand increases and interest rates decrease. When real GDP increases, there is a greater demand for money for transactions and speculative purposes. The money demand curve increases, shifts rightward, and interest rates increase as we move up along the money supply curve.
   False

Problems: government Bank

1. The central bank of Aviator Lake decides it wants to increase the money supply.   MS.
   a) What might have prompted this decision?
      - Recessionary gap. When real GDP < Potential GDP
        $\uparrow$ MS to $\uparrow$ AD & move Y to Y*
   b) How would the central bank go about doing this?
      - Central bank buys bonds in open market operations. (buy bonds in public)
      - Central bank could reduce the bank rate. (decrease interest rate)
      - Central bank reduces the overnight loans rate. ~~Price~~

   c) On the following diagrams, show the process by which the money supply increases.   higher i, buy less

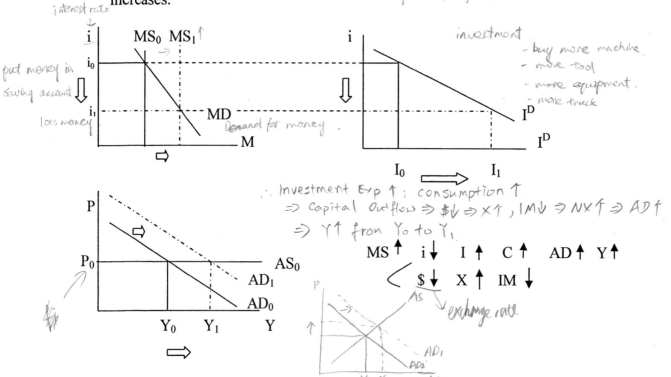

   Investment Exp $\uparrow$; consumption $\uparrow$
   $\Rightarrow$ Capital outflow $\Rightarrow$ $\$\downarrow$ $\Rightarrow$ X$\uparrow$, IM$\downarrow$ $\Rightarrow$ NX$\uparrow$ $\Rightarrow$ AD$\uparrow$
   $\Rightarrow$ Y$\uparrow$ from Y_0 to Y_1.

   MS $\uparrow$ i$\downarrow$ I $\uparrow$ C $\uparrow$ AD$\uparrow$ Y$\uparrow$
   $\langle$ $\$\downarrow$ X $\uparrow$ IM $\downarrow$
   exchange rate

   d) Does desired investment expenditure change? Explain.
      MS $\uparrow$ i $\downarrow$ I $\uparrow$ Yes.

e) Is the Aviator Lake dollar affected in any way? Explain.

MS ↑ i ↓   interest rate ↓ go to Canada

⤵ C $ ↓ Canada

f) Are there any changes in net exports? Explain.

MS ↑ i ↓

⤵ C$ ↓ → X ↑ IM ↓ } NX ↑

g) Do aggregate demand and real GDP change? Explain. Yes

investment I ↑   NX ↑   AD ↑   Y ↑

i low

2. The bank of Aviator Lake decides it wants to decrease the money supply.

a) What might have prompted this decision?
- Inflationary gap. when real GDP > Potential GDP.

b) How would the central bank go about doing this?
- Central bank sells bonds in open market operations.   – sell bonds.
- Central bank could increase the bank rate.   – Increase interest rates
- Central bank could increase overnight loans rate.

c) On the following diagrams, show the process by which the money supply decreases.

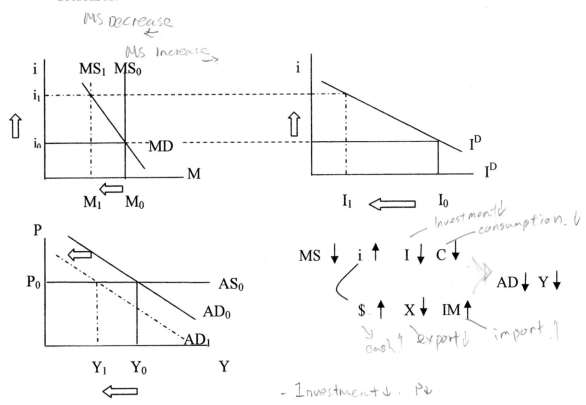

MS Decrease

MS Increase →

MS ↓ i ↑ I ↓ C ↓

Investment ↓
consumption ↓

AD ↓ Y ↓

$ ↑ X ↓ IM ↑

cash ↑ export ↓ import ↑

- Investment ↓. P↓

d) Does desired investment expenditure change? Explain.

MS $\downarrow$ i $\uparrow$ I $\downarrow$

e) Is the Aviator Lake dollar affected in any way? Explain.

MS $\downarrow$ i $\uparrow$

$\quad\quad\quad$ $\langle$ $ \uparrow$

f) Are there any changes in net exports? Explain.

MS $\downarrow$ i $\uparrow$

$\quad\quad$ $\langle$ C$\uparrow$ X $\downarrow$ IM $\uparrow$ }   NX $\downarrow$

g) Do aggregate demand and real GDP change? Explain.

$\quad$ I $\downarrow$ NX $\downarrow$ AD $\downarrow$ Y $\downarrow$

3. The money market is presently not in equilibrium. The interest rates are at a high level. Discuss the relationship between the interest rates and the price of bonds.

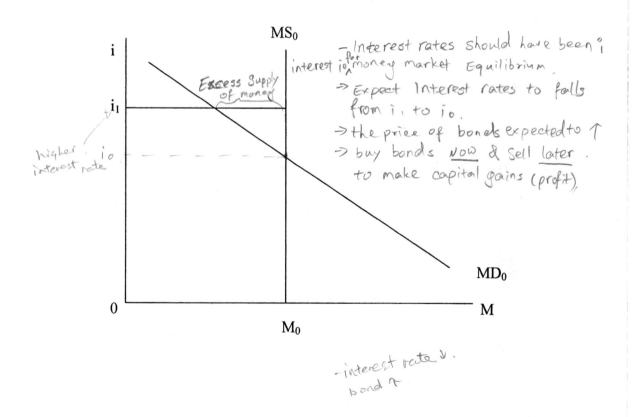

MS₀

i

i₁

Excess Supply of money

higher interest rate   i₀

0   M₀   MD₀   M

- Interest rates should have been ? interest i₀ for money market Equilibrium.
⟹ Expect Interest rates to falls from i₁ to i₀.
⟹ the price of bonds expected to ↑
⟹ buy bonds NOW & Sell later. to make capital gains (profit)

- interest rate ↓.
  bond ↑

- At high rates of interest, we expect interest rates to decline.

- Excess supply of money.

- Opportunity cost of holding money is high.

- Buy bonds.

- Expect capital gains. *profit*

- Draw down cash balances.

- $i \downarrow$ $P_B \uparrow$

4. The money market is presently not in equilibrium. The interest rates are at a low level. Discuss the relationship between the interest rates and the price of bonds, the need for cash balances, and the opportunity cost for holding money.

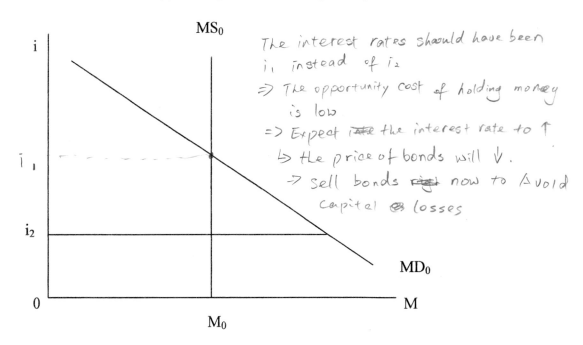

The interest rates should have been i_1 instead of i_2
⟹ The opportunity cost of holding money is low
⟹ Expect the interest rate to ↑
↳ the price of bonds will ↓.
⟶ sell bonds now to Avoid capital losses

- At low rates of interest, we expect interest rates to rise.

- Excess demand for money.

- Opportunity cost of holding money is low.

- Sell bonds.

- Avoid capital losses.

- Drive up cash balances.

- $i \uparrow$ $P_B \downarrow$

(5.) Show the monetary transmission mechanism as part of open market operations if the money supply was increased.

Monetary Transmission Mechanism:

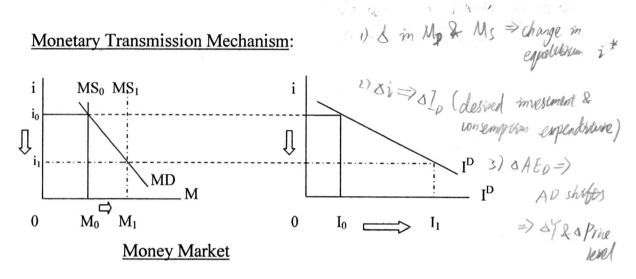

1) Δ in M_D & M_S ⇒ change in equilibrium i^*

2) Δi ⇒ ΔI_D (desired investment & consumption expenditure)

3) $\Delta A E_D$ ⇒ AD shifts

⇒ ΔY & Δ Price level

Money Market

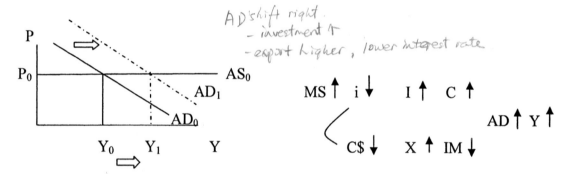

AD's shift right.
- investment ↑
- export higher, lower interest rate

MS ↑   i ↓   I ↑   C ↑

C$ ↓   X ↑   IM ↓   AD ↑ Y ↑

Goods or Output Market

Any changes that occur in the money market, that is, changes in the money supply or interest rates, affect investment expenditures; and they in turn cause changes in the output or goods market, that is, aggregate demand and real GDP.

76

6. Using the money-market diagrams, show why monetary policy is more effective with a monetarist approach.

With the same given change in the money supply:

Keynesian:

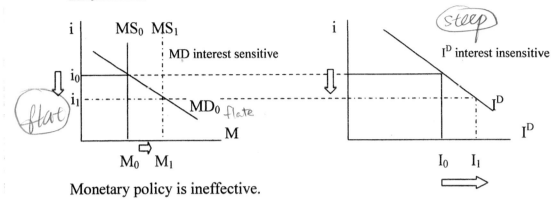

Monetary policy is ineffective.

Monetarist:

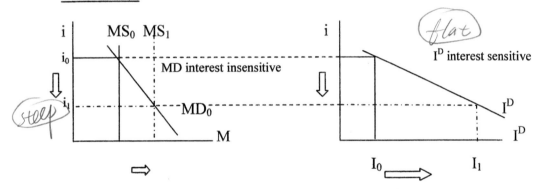

Monetary policy is very effective.

Monetary policy is ineffective from a Keynesian viewpoint because the change in investment expenditures is small; however, looking at the same change in the money supply from a monetarist perspective, the change in investment expenditures is large making monetary policy very effective.

*Note: Monetarists view the money demand curve as steep or interest insensitive while the investment demand curve is viewed as flat or interest rate sensitive. With any given change in the money supply, this leads to a greater change in the interest rate and a greater change in investment expenditures.

Chapter 28

1. $$PV = \frac{FV}{(1+i)^T}$$

⇒ The price of a bond is inversely related to the interest rate.

2. The demand for money, $MD = MD(\bar{i}, \overset{+}{Y}, \overset{+}{P})$.

3. The monetary Transmission mechanism!

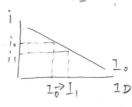

M (quantity of money)

i ⇒ interest rate.

I → Investment

consumption ↑
- Capital outflow: → $ ↓ (currency Depreci...
  ⇒ X↑; IM↓; NX
  ⇒ AD↑ ⇒ Y↑

Assignment #8: Monetary Policy in Canada

Multiple Choice:

1. Which of the following is **not** one of the four functions of money?   [c]
   a) medium of exchange
   b) standard of deferred payment
   c) measure of liquidity *how quickly convert. asset of cash*
   d) store of value
   e) unit of account

   Commercial bank
2. A bank can create money by   [d]
   a) printing more cheques.
   b) increasing its reserves.
   c) selling some of its bonds.
   d) lending its <u>excess reserves.</u> *over and above the legal og*
   e) converting reserves into bonds.

True/False:

↑ get cash

1. If the Bank of Canada wanted to <u>decrease the money supply,</u> it would <u>sell bonds</u> in open market operations.
   - Bank of Canada would sell bonds in open market operations.
   - Reserves decrease.
   - Excess reserves decrease.
   - Loans decrease.
   - Money supply decreases.
   True

Discussion Questions:

1. Describe the target that the Central Bank of Canada (BOC) sets for <u>overnight interest rates</u> (or, overnight loans rate).
   The target interest rate is the midpoint of a 0.5% point range within which the Bank would like to see the actual overnight interest rate.

2. When the BOC sets its target for the overnight interest rate, what other two rates does it set?
   It sets: 1. The bank rate -- the upper band – the rate at which they are willing to lend.
   2. The bankers deposit rate – the lower band – the rate at which they are willing to pay interest.

79

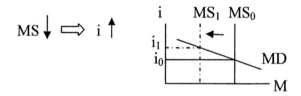

3. Why is changing the <u>money supply</u> an ineffective way of conducting monetary policy?

When the central bank attempts to shift the money supply directly, it <u>changes</u> the equilibrium <u>rate of interest</u>. The central bank cannot directly, precisely control the money supply and the slope of money demand is to some degree uncertain.

4. State the <u>three reasons</u> why the central bank does not implement policy in this manner.
   1. It <u>cannot control</u> <u>cash reserves</u> through open market operations.
   2. It <u>cannot control</u> the <u>process of deposit</u> expansion by the commercial banks.
   3. The money supply equals deposits plus currency. The central bank can influence the money supply but, it cannot control it.

      MS = MD + currency

      CB can influence, but cannot control it.

Problems:

1. In open market operations, the central bank sells $100 million in government bonds.
   a) Do the commercial bank reserves change? If they change, by how much do they change? In which direction would they change?

   $\Delta R \downarrow = -100$ million   *reserves ↓*

   b) If the <u>money multiplier</u> were given as 5, would there be a change in the money supply? If so, by how much would it change? In which direction would it change?

   $\Delta MS = mm * \Delta R$
   $= 5 * -100$ ↓ MS
   $= -500$ million

   c) Would the interest rates change? (Direction and diagram) *Yes*

   The BOC would increase the overnight loans rate.

   i ↑   MD ↑

   To accommodate the increase in interest rates, the BOC would sell bonds in open market operations.

   MS ↓ ⇒ i ↑

d) Would aggregate demand be affected? Why?

$\implies$ AD $\downarrow$

e) Would real GDP change?

AD $\downarrow$ $\Big\}$ $\implies$ Y $\downarrow$
AE $\downarrow$

2. The central bank buys $100 million in bonds from private households in open market operations. The target reserves are 10%.
   a) Show the *immediate* effects on the T-accounts following.

Private Households

Assets		Liabilities
Bonds	−$100	No change
Deposits	+ $100	

Commercial Banks

Assets		Liabilities	
Reserves	+100	Demand Deposits	+100

Central Bank

Assets		Liabilities	
Bonds	+100	Commercial bank deposits or Reserves of commercial banks	+100

b) What would the commercial banks do now, given that their target reserves must be addressed?

Reserves $= 0.1 \ast + \$100 = + \$10$

Excess reserves or loans $= \$100 - \$10 = + \$90$

c) Do these actions affect overall change in deposits and the money supply? Explain.

$\Delta D = DM \ast \Delta D$ (immediate) or $\Delta MS = DM \ast \Delta R$ (immediate)

ΔD or $\Delta MS = \dfrac{1}{0.1} \ast + \$100 = + \$1{,}000$ ⇧

($\Delta D = \Delta R$ -- this refers to the immediate change) $DM = \dfrac{1}{V} = \dfrac{1}{.1} = 10$

*Note: You must always state the direction of the change.

3. Redo the same question as #2; however, all private household funds are now held as deposits in the commercial banks.
*Note: Only two T-accounts are now used: the T-account for the commercial banks and the T-account for the central bank.

a) Show the *immediate* effects on the T-accounts following.

Commercial Banks

Assets		Liabilities	
Reserves	+100	Demand Deposits	+100
Bonds	−100		

Central Bank

Assets		Liabilities	
Bonds	+100	Commercial bank deposits +100	
		or Reserves of commercial banks	

b) What would the commercial banks do now, given that their target reserves must be addressed?

$$\text{Reserves} = 0.1 * \$100 = +\$10$$
$$\text{Excess reserves or Loans} = \$100 - \$10 = +\$90$$

c) Do these actions affect overall change in deposits and the money supply? Explain.

$$\Delta D = DM * \Delta D \text{ (immediate)} \quad \text{or} \quad \Delta MS = DM * \Delta R \text{ (immediate)}$$
$$\Delta D \text{ or } \Delta MS = \frac{1}{0.1} * +\$100 = +\$1,000 \Uparrow$$

($\Delta D = \Delta R$ -- this refers to the immediate change)
*Note: You must always state the direction of the change.

82

4. With the current interest rate, commercial banks are in need of more cash. There is a growing demand for loans; however, the commercial banks are fully loaned out. The central bank is buying $1,000 in bonds from the commercial banks in open market operations. (Commercial banks are selling bonds.)

a) Show the *immediate* effects on the T-accounts following.

Commercial Banks

Assets		Liabilities
Reserves	+1000	No change
Bonds	−1000	

(Only the form of the assets change but, that does not change the total assets or liabilities.

Cash reserves increase making more loans available.)

Central Bank

Assets		Liabilities	
Bonds	+1000	Currency in circulation	+1000

(Overall currency in the economy is increased.)

b) Discuss the expansion of the money supply that would follow if the target reserve ratio is 10 percent?

$$DM = \frac{1}{v} = \frac{1}{0.1} = 10 \qquad \Delta MS = DM * \Delta R$$

$$\Delta MS = 10 * + 1,000$$

$$\Delta MS = + 10,000 \; \Uparrow$$

Lends out $1,000.

c) If all banks in the banking system keep reserves of 10 percent and there is a cash drain of 10 percent, what would be the expected expansion in the money supply?

$$\Delta MS = mm * \Delta R \text{ (immediate)} \qquad mm = \frac{1}{v + c}$$

$$\Delta MS = \frac{1}{\underset{reserves}{v} + \underset{cash \, drain}{c}} = \frac{1}{0.1 + 0.1} = \frac{1}{0.2} * + \$1000 = + \$5,000 \quad \Uparrow$$

*Note: mm is the money multiplier.

5. The economy of Aviator Lake is experiencing a recessionary gap. The central bank of Aviator Lake decides to target overnight loans.
   a) How would the central bank of Aviator Lake go about doing this?
      - Reduce the overnight loans rate.
        This in turn would reduce the interest rate and cause an accommodation by the central bank of Aviator Lake to buy bonds in open market operations.
   b) On the following diagrams, show the process by which the money market adjusts.

money.

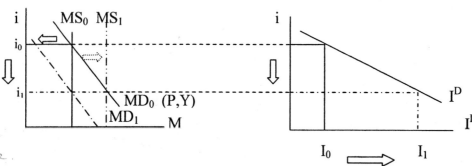

goods & service.

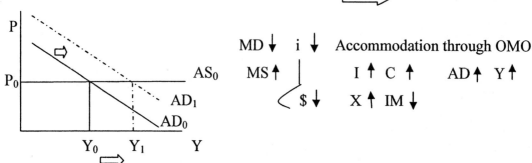

MD ↓ i ↓ Accommodation through OMO

MS ↑ | I ↑ C ↑ AD ↑ Y ↑

$ ↓ X ↑ IM ↓

   c) Does desired investment expenditure change? Explain.
      i ↓ I ↑ Investments are interest sensitive and negatively related to the interest rate. As interest rates decline, durable goods are less expensive.

   d) Is the Aviator Lake dollar affected in any way? Explain.
      i ↓ Lower interest rates cause capital outflows from the economy.

      $ ↓ The Aviator Lake dollar is sold internationally and its value declines.

   e) Are there any changes in net exports? Explain.
      i ↓ The capital outflows cause a decline in the Aviator Lake dollar which makes goods from Aviator Lake cheaper and exports increase. The cheaper dollar decreases imports.

      $ ↓ X ↑ IM ↓ } NX ↑

   f) Do aggregate demand and real GDP change? Explain.
      I ↑ NX ↑ AD ↑ Y ↑